Investing in Brazil Stocks

Investing in Brazil Stocks:

Get Rich from the South American Giant

By Fred Fuld III

Publishing Division
Investment Research Institute™
5100 Clayton Road, Suite B-1, #405
Concord CA 94521 USA
www.InvestmentResearchInstitute.com

ISBN 978-0-6151-9697-8

First edition.

Acknowledgements

To James Altucher, who helped me get heavily into financial writing.

To Jim Cramer, who validated my opinion of Brazilian stocks.

To Ronnie Nogueira, at Revista RI Magazine, and Marita Graça Feijó Bittencourt and Rodrigo Alvarez, at Globo TV, all of whom made me famous in Brazil.

To Gisele Bündchen, who has helped companies in Brazil and around the world become more successful through her endorsements.

Table of Contents

Brazil Food Stocks

Brazil Utility & Forestry Stocks

Brazil Airline Stocks

Introduction

The country of Brazil provides an unbelievable opportunity for investors. Brazil has a hard working population, a stable democracy, very extensive natural resources and dozens of publicly traded companies which trade on the New York Stock Exchange.

The term BRIC, which stands for Brazil, Russia, India, and China, is generally attributed to Goldman Sachs, and refers to the fastest growing emerging markets in the world. The thesis proposed by Goldman Sachs is that by the year 2050, these four countries will be the global leaders in terms of economies.

Of the four countries, the country of Brazil, officially known as the República Federativa do Brasil, which has been a republic since 1889 and a

> **Brazil is the fifth largest country in the world by both population & area**

steady democracy since 1988, has by far the greatest potential for economic growth. Brazil, which is the fifth largest country in the world by both population and area, has the eighth highest gross domestic product on a purchasing power parity basis, according to the International Monetary Fund (they are ranked tenth by the CIA World Fact Book and the World Bank).

The country has an enormous amount of natural resources. They are the largest producer of oil and

> **Brazil has the largest Japanese population outside of Japan**

gas in South America. As a matter of fact, at the end of 2007, a huge deepwater oil field was discovered off the coast of Brazil, which is expected to have as much as 8 billion barrels of light crude oil, and would make it one of the largest oil fields in the world.

However, Brazil is also the largest producer of ethanol in the world, which they produce from sugarcane. They export 700 million gallons of ethanol a year. This bio-energy superpower was helped along by the Programa Nacional do Álcool, also known as Pró-Álcool, the government financed program to replace gasoline with ethanol for automobiles. This program, which went into effect in 1975, helped reduce the number of gasoline operated cars by 10 million. Brazil is also becoming a leader in biodiesel, which can be created from almost any type of vegetable oil. The growth of soybean farmland has almost doubled to accommodate the production.

In its effort to reduce its dependence on fossil fuels, Brazil has produced more hydro generated electricity in the world than any other country except Canada and China, amounting to 83% of all electricity that they produce. With strides like these, Brazil may become the greenest country in the world.

In addition to ethanol, other exports include aircraft, automobiles, beef, coffee, iron ore, orange juice, soybeans, steel, and textiles. As a matter of fact, it is a net exporter. The service industry is also strong, especially the banking industry which reportedly makes up 16% of the GDP.

The literacy rate has been running around 88% for the entire population and over 93% for teenagers. The strong literacy is due to the fact that 18% of federal taxes and 25%

of state and local taxes are allocated towards education. The official high school curriculum includes classes in English.

Investment Features of Brazil:

1. Their GDP is the highest in Latin America, in excess of a trillion dollars.
2. When Brazil received an IMF rescue loan in 2002, they paid it off a year earlier than when it was due.
3. It is the largest producer of ethanol in the world.
4. It is the third largest producer of hydro power in the world.
5. It owns the world largest hydroelectric power plant based on electricity generation.
6. It is the fourth largest democracy in the world.
7. Mineral resources include nickel, tin, chromites, bauxite, beryllium, gold, copper, lead, tungsten, zinc, and coal.
8. Foreign direct investment averages $20 billion per year.
9. It has over 100 trading partners.
10. It is the South American leader in space research.and participated in the the construction of the International Space Station.
11. 73% of its oil reserves are extracted through deep water.
12. GDP growth for 2007 was 5.1%.

Gisele Bündchen Stock Index

The supermodel superstar Gisele Bündchen is rich, intelligent, beautiful and financially savvy, just like Brazil, the country she is from. She was named by Forbes magazine as the top earning supermodel, earning $33 million in 2006. According to Guinness World Records, Gisele is now the richest supermodel in the world. She is of German ancestry on both her mother's and father's side and she has a twin sister names Patricia.

I have developed a series of celebrity stock indices during the last year, specializing in actresses, singers and supermodels. Because Gisele is connected to several publicly traded companies, I developed the Gisele Bündchen Stock Index. For the year 2007, the Gisele Index was up 29%, substantially outperforming the Dow Jones Industrial Average which was up only 6.5% during the same period.

What is interesting to note is that when Gisele terminated her agreement back in May of 2007 with Victoria's Secret, which is owned by Limited Brands Inc. (LTD), Limited was selling for $26.80 per share. By the end of the year, the stock dropped by over 30% from the date that Gisele departed from Limited.

Gisele can have extensive influence on the revenues of companies. When C&A Brazil, a division of C&A, which is an international chain of clothing stores, hired her to appear in their television commercials, the company's revenues increased by 30%. In addition, she reportedly earned $6 million a year by licensing her name to Grendene, a Brazilian shoe company. Companies don't pay that much money out of the goodness of their hearts; they expect their earnings to increase significantly enough to substantially more than cover the cost of the celebrity endorsement fee.

Gisele has been the face of numerous advertising campaigns, including Apple Inc. (AAPL), appearing on the 'Get a Mac' advertisements to promote their new line of Macintosh computers. Speaking of Macs, a different kind of Mac, Gisele was supposedly discovered by a modeling agent while eating a Big Mac hamburger at a local McDonald's when she was fourteen years old.

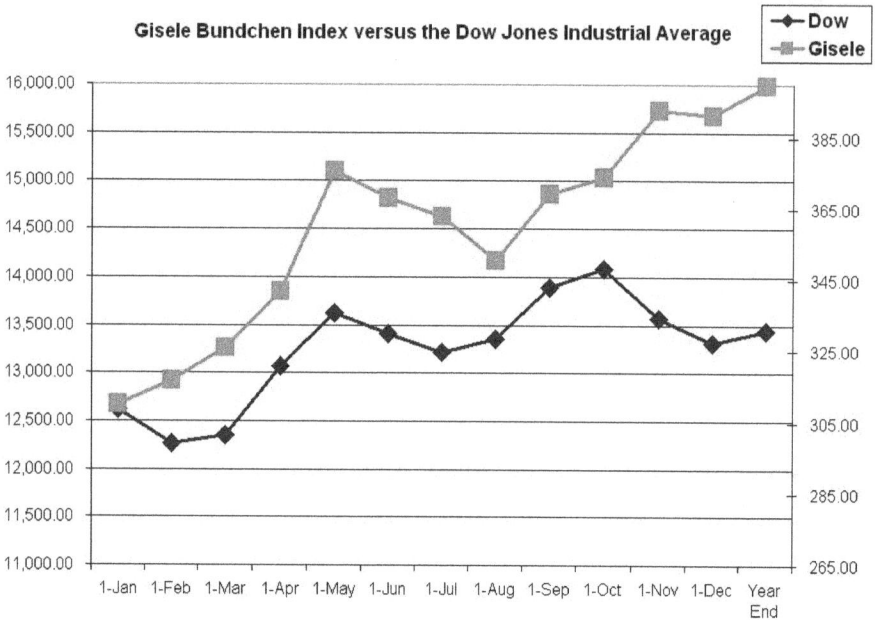

Gisele Bundchen Index versus the Dow Jones Industrial Average

Although Victoria's Secret recently announced in May that Gisele had ended her contract with them, she had been one of their main models for several years and the primary face for many of their advertising campaigns. Victoria's Secret is owned by Limited Brands (LTD).

Gisele has also been a celebrity endorser for Ralph Lauren, which is owned by Polo Ralph Lauren Corp. (RL).

Vivo Participacoes S.A. (VIV), the largest mobile phone service provider in Brazil and in South America, is another company that Gisele did a celebrity endorsement for.

News Corp. (NWS) is another company she is connected with. She starred in the comedy, Taxi, in her movie debut, and The Devil Wears Prada , both produced by 20th Century Fox, a division of News Corp.

She is rumored to be starring in the upcoming Angels and Demons movie distributed by Sony (SNE).

She won the the VH1/Vogue Model of the Year, VH1 owned by MTV Networks, which is owned by Viacom, Inc. (VIA-B).

LVMH Moët Hennessy Louis Vuitton S.A. (LVMUY.PK) owns several companies which Gisele is the spokesperson for, including Louis Vuitton (a luxury French fashion company), Givenchy (French retailer of clothing, accessories, perfumes and cosmetics), Guerlain (the oldest perfume house in the world), and Céline.

She also did an advertising campaign face for Bulgari (BULIF.PK), the Italian jeweler and luxury goods retailer.

In addition, she was the celebrity endorser for Balenciaga, a fashion house, which is owned by Gucci, which is owned by PPR SA (PPRUF.PK).

Lagardere Groupe SCA (LGDDF.PK) owns ELLE magazine, on which and in which Gisele's picture appeared many times.

It appears that it may be time to change the components of the index since Gisele recently signed a contract with Procter & Gamble Co. (PG) to promote their Pantene hair products. In addition, she is also working with Disney (DIS), dressed as Wendy from Peter Pan. Let's hope her index keeps on rising.

Brazil Chemical, Energy and Mining Stocks

Braskem S.A. (BAK)

Braskem S.A. is Brazil's largest petrochemical company, with a substantial portion of its shares owned by Odebrecht and Petrobras. The company has the largest research complex for their industry in Latin America, which is located in Truinfo, in the state of Rio Grande do Sul. The company's shares are listed on the NYSE Euronext, Sao Paulo, and Madrid stock exchanges. Currently, Braskem has 3,300 employee and is headquartered out of Sao Paulo. In addition, the company has offices in Argentina, Bahia, Maranhao, Minas Gerais, Parana, Pernambuco, Santa Catarina, Rio de Janeiro, Sao Paolo, the Netherlands, the United States and Venezuela.

History

The history of Braskem began in 1972 when the company was founded as Petroquimica do Nordeste Copene Ltd. The company would go on to change its name two years later to Copene Petroquimica do Nordeste S.A.

Thirty years later, the company would go through its next major change when it merged with OPP, Trikem, Nitrocarbono, Proppet e Polialden and Odebrecht in the creation of a new company, Braskem S.A. in 2002. This merger was due to a major reconstruction in the Brazilian petrochemical industry. The merger was dominated by Odebrecht, which is a heavy engineering and construction company owned by the Odebrecht family. Four years later, the company acquired Politeno, which is a producer of polyethylene in Camacari. In 2007, the company acquired the Ipiranga Group and developed the first "green" polyethylene in the world.

Profile

The business of Braskem is split into four operating divisions, each corresponding to a principal production process of its products: Basic Petrochemicals Unit, Polyolefin Unit, Vinyl Unit and the Business Development Unit.

The Basic Petrochemicals Unit produces several different petrochemicals, including ethylene, polymer and chemical grade propylene, butadiene, isoprene and butane-1, benzene, toluene, para-xylene and ortho-xylene.

These products are mostly used to create petrochemical products, including those produced by other business units in the company. The company's operations in this business unit operate at the petrochemical complex in Camacari, located in the Brazilian state of Bahia. This is often referred to as their Northeastern Complex. The facilities located in the Northeastern Complex also generate thermoelectric power, water treatment and the production of steam and compressed air. The company generates 70 percent of the power it needs in the Northeastern complex, itself. The rest of the power is sold to Companhia Hidro Electrica do Sao Francisco, which is a government-owned electric power generation company.

The Polyolefin Unit produces such products as polyethylene, low-density polyethylene, linear low-density polyethylene, high-density polyethylene and ultra-high molecular-weight polyethylene, and polypropylene. The polyolefin that is manufactured by Braskem is used in a wide variety of products for both industries and consumers, including packaging, shopping bags, bottles, automotive parts and household appliances.

All of the polyolefin products manufactured by Braskem are made in their facilities at the Northeastern Complex, in addition to their petrochemical complex in Truinfo, in the state of Rio Grande do Sul. This area is often referred to as Southern Complex. The acquisition of Politeno added six new grades of polyethylene to the Polyolefin Unit.

In 2006, the company launched its Idealis resin, which is a molecular-weight polyethylene used in equipment for the food and automotive industries. That same year, it developed polypropylene with nanoparticles, which is the first resin in Brazil to be based on nanotechnology. As of the end of 2006, Braskem had nine polyolefin facilities, five of which are located in the Southern Complex. Combined, they have an annual production capacity of over 30,000 tons per plant.

The Vinyl Unit of Braskem is responsible for one of the largest PVC production capacities in Latin America and the only vertically integrated producer of PVC in Brazil, and it is integrated through its production of chlorine and other raw materials. The Vinyl Unit also manufactures caustic soda, used in the production of aluminum, chlorine, ethylene dichloride and paper.

In June of 2007, Braskem had a 53 percent share of the Brazilian PVC market because the company manufactured a wide range of industrial products that are used in the construction industry, including pipes, sheeting, flooring, fittings and wire and cable coverings. In addition to household products, the company manufactures plastic films, packaging materials, synthetic leather, window frames and bottles, which are produced in facilities in the states of Bahia, Alagoas and Sao Paulo.

The Business Development Unit of Braskem is responsible for manufacturing products such as polyethylene teraphthalate [PET] and caprolactam. PET is used to make soft drinks, medications, cleaning products, mineral water and other food products. Caprolactam is used to make Nylon-

6 textile thread, engineering resins and film, along with structural material for the motor and electronic industries. This division also produces ammonium sulfate, which is a primary ingrediant in fertilizer. In the company's factories, the business unit of Braskem also produces cyclohexane and cyclohexanone, which is used in paint solvents, pesticides, oils, rubber and other industrial products.

This unit of Braskem also manages various aspects of the company's investments. As of the end of 2006, the Business Development Unit had a production capacity of 78,000 tons of PET and 62,000 tons of caprolactam.

In total, the company operates 13 chemical plants, which have a combined production capacity of roughly five million tons per year. These plants are located in three primary complexes, Camacari in the state of Bahia, Truinfo in the state of Rio Grande do Sul, and a plant in Sao Paulo State, with other plants located in Alagoas. The company's main focus is thermoplastic resins, but it also produces half of Brazil's output of basic petrochemicals and solvents.

Braskem was one of ten winners of the Destaques Cias Abertas Award, which is an award promoted by the Estado Group for good performance in the capital market from the standpoint of the investor. There were 149 participants for this award from eight different industries. The awards criteria included: price/earnings, price/equity value of shares, fluctuation, liquidity, volatility, dividends/equity value and return on shareholder's equity.

Recent News

Braskem made major headlines in June of 2007 when they announced they had created 100 percent renewable polyethylene, which is derived primarily from ethanol, something that Brazil has a substantial amount of. The company announced that they would be producing the product by 2009, at the earliest.

Also, Braskem announced it would be taking part in a joint effort with a methane plant in Bolivia, owned by Yacimientos Petroliferos Fiscales Bolivianos, with an investment between $750 million and $1 billion over three years.

In December of 2007, Braskem announced it would be installing a modern and competitive petrochemical project in Venezuela, as part of a joint effort with Pequiven at a cost of almost $3.5 billion.

<u>Companhia Siderurgica Nacional</u> <u>(SID)</u>

Companhia Siderurgica Nacional, also known as CSN, is the second largest steel-maker in Brazil and has its main plant located in the city of Volta Redonda in the state of Rio de Janiero. The company is the largest full-integrated steel producer in Brazil, and is one of the largest crude steel producers in Latin America. With regards to capacity, it has a crude steel capacity and rolled product capacity of over five million tons each year. Approximately 49 percent of the galvanized steel products sold in Brazil are generated by this company. The CEO of the company is Benjamin Steinbruch.

The headquarters for the company is located in Rio De Janeiro, while the company has factories located in the Vale do Paraiba region. The company also has iron mines at Congonhas and Arcos, and coal mines at Sideropolis and Santa Catarina.

Offices are also located in Sao Paulo, Volta Redonda, Araucaria, Porto Real, Maracanau, Terre Huate in the United States, Paio Pires in Portugal, and Congonhas, Itaguai, Arcos, Fortaleza and Ita in Brazil. The company has over 13,000 employees.

History

The company began as a state-owned company on April 9, 1941 after an agreement was reached between the American and Brazilian governments to build a plant that would manufacture steel for the Allies during World War II.

In 1946, it began its operations under Presidente Eurico Gaspar Dutra. It was originally called the Presidente

Vargas Steelworks, due to the fact that the decree for the company's creation was issued under the presidency of Getulio Vargas. The factory started out producing coke, pig iron casting and long products before two expansions took place in the 1970s. The first increased annual production capacity to 1.6 million tons of crude steel in 1974, and the second, three years later, increased the capacity to 2.4 million tons. In 1989, the capacity was increased to 4.5 million tons of crude steel.

In 1993, CSN ceased to be a government entity. That year, a series of auctions were held in which the Brazilian government sold off 91 percent of the company to the public.

That same year, CSN had adopted a capital improvement program which was extended in 1995. The goals for this program were outlined as an increase in the production of crude steel, improving the productivity of production units, and enhancing the environmental protection and cleanup program.

In 1996, the company expanded its operations to the industry of infrastructure with its participation in two hydroelectric plants. In 1997, the company reached the historic mark of producing 100 million tons of steel. In 2001, a process of internationalization began for CSN when they purchased American Heartland Steel.

Then in 2004, CSN announced they would be investing $820 million through 2007 for the expansion of annual production of the Casa de Pedra iron ore mine, the expansion of the coal terminal adjacent to the Sepetiba port and the construction of a six million-ton pellet plant.

Profile

Companhia Siderurgica Nacional produces carbon steel, in addition to many other types of steel products, which are used internationally as a primary raw material for several industries, including the automotive, home appliance, packaging, and construction industries. CSN also produces limestone, dolomite, and tin.

The company also creates tin mill products, including tin plate, tin-free steel, low-tin coated steel and black plate products. Also, the company maintains investments in railroads and power supply companies. It sells its steel products throughout Brazil and 71 other countries around the world, utilizing its sale force and distributors.

As one of the top steel-makers in the world, the company produces six million tons of raw steel and five million tons of laminates each year.

Several firms are also owned by CSN, including GalvaSud and Inal. The company also has container and coal terminals in the Itaguai port, while controlling MRS Logistics, CFN, railroads and hydroelectric dams through its shareholdings. CSN also has factories in the United States and Portugal.

However, there is the possibility that future regulations from the government could have a negative impact on the company's earnings. These measures include protectionist measures from the government which could affect export sales and environmental standards that are being imposed on

> **CSN produces 98 percent of all the tin mill products sold in Brazil**

CSN, which makes their steel-making facilities subject to new laws and regulations.

CSN may be looking at higher taxes since the Brazilian Federal Congress amended the Brazilian Constitution, which may affect the profit margins of the company.

The earnings of CSN are also heavily affected by the fluctuations of the exchange rate.

Company News

On June 5, 2006, the company acquired Companhia Metalurgica Prada, and subsequently on August 31, 2006, CSN acquired half of Lusosider Projectos Siderurgicos. In July 2007, CSN acquired Companhia de Fomento Mineral. On Dec. 18 of that year, CSN announced an investment of $5.2 billion until 2011 in steel, cement and mining in the southern state of Minas Gerais in Brazil. The main mine, Casa de Pedra, will increase production capacity from its current 16 million tons of iron ore to 65 million tons in just six years. A new plant will also be built there, at a cost of $3.4 billion, which will produce 4.5 million tons of steel per year.

In 2006, a heated bidding war erupted between Tata Steel and CSN over the acquisition of Corus, the Anglo-Dutch steel firm, valued at $9.6 billion. A deal between Tata Steel and Corus was nearly finalized before CSN submitted a competing offer on Nov. 17. On Jan. 30, 2007, Tata Steel and CSN submitted new bids for Corus in an auction. The India based Tata Steel ended up being the successful bidder.

Trivia

In 2004, CSN accounted for 98 percent of all the tin mill products sold in Brazil, making it one of the world's leading producers of tin mill products.

A total of 39 percent of the exports that come out of the company are shipped to the United States, with the second closest being Europe at 35 percent. Asia accounts for 13 percent and only 10 percent of the exports from the company stay in South America.

Companhia Vale do Rio Doce (RIO)

Companhia Vale do Rio Doce is a multinational mining corporation which is the second largest mining company in the world and the largest logistics operator in Brazil. In addition to being a world leader in the production of manganese, copper, bauxite, potash, kaolin and aluminum, Vale is also the largest producer in the world of iron ore, pellets and nickel.

While Vale is headquartered in Rio de Janeiro, it has offices on every continent but Antarctica, and 16 Brazilian states. Since its inception, Vale has participated in mining operations in Finland, Canada, Australia, Mongolia, China, India, Angola, South Africa, Chile and Peru, In addition as many other countries. Other offices for the company are located in Tokyo, Buenos Aires, Seoul, Lima, Toronto, London, Johannesburg, Singapore and Shanghai. Currently, the company has over 100,000 employees.

History

Founded in Itabira, a Brazilian Municipal District, on June 1, 1942, the company rose quickly in terms of prominence and business growth. Only one year after the Vitoria a Minas railroad was inaugurated and seven years after Vale was created, the company was responsible for 80 percent of Brazilian iron ore exports.

By 1966, the company began operations in Espirito Santa, one of the most important ports for the company. One of the company's significant holdings is the Carajas Mine.

The mine currently has 1.5 billion tons of iron ore in reserve. Vale has been the biggest exporter of iron ore since 1974.

On Dec. 11, 1982, Vale suffered a huge loss when its headquarters were nearly destroyed by a fire that was caused by an electrical short on the 15th floor of the building. That same year, Vale diversified into producing aluminum in Rio de Janeiro. In addition, the company expanded its efforts out of the southeast, where it has traditionally worked, into the northeast, central-west, and north of Brazil. This in turn has allowed it to expand its mineral product portfolio and consolidate logistic services.

On May 6, 1997, Vale was privatized when the Brazil Consortium aquired 41.73 percent of the government's stock for $3.14 billion. This decision caused a great deal of controversy, and there were some politicians who opposed the privatization.

From its inception in 1942, Vale has risen to have a market capitalization of $180 billion, which is due in large part to their massive mineral exploration efforts in a total of 19 countries worldwide.

In 2007, it was a significant year for the company, beginning with the purchase of Inco, the Canadian nickel mining company, a world leader in nickel producing. The purchase was completed on Jan. 30, helping Vale to earn a BBB rating by Standard and Poor's on Feb. 13.

On May 2, Vale signed the contract to build the four biggest bulk carriers in the world, each having a capacity of 388,000 tons. The company also announced on Sept. 24 the plan to plant 346 million trees until 2010, which would be the largest re-vegetation and environmental preservation project in Latin America.

Profile

The business sector of Vale is based in large part on its mining operations, which are split into three different systems in Brazil: the Southeastern System, the Southern System and the Northern System.

The Southeastern System is in the state of Minas Gerais, where there are three significant mining areas: Itabira, Centrais Mines and Mariana. In these mines, iron ore is taken out by using an open-pit method. A very interesting aspect about the company's power plants in the Southeastern System is that the electrical energy consumed by them is 100 percent produced by Vale, through the methods of crushing, classification and concentration to produce sinter feed.

In the Southern System, located in Minas Gerais and Rio de Janeiro, iron ore is transported by MRS Logistica to the Guaiba Island and Itaguai maritime terminals, both located in the city of Rio de Janeiro. In 2006, Vale produced 22 percent of the electrical energy consumed in the Southern Sector.

The Nothern System for Vale is made up of an ore-processing complex, with open-pit mines in the Carajas region. The reserves here are considered to be some of the largest in the world, with incredibly high iron content, 70 percent, in the deposits. As a result of the high iron content, Vale does not have to operate a concentration plant at Carajas. Through using a mining process of sizing operations that include crushing and filtration, Vale is able to produce iron for the market in this region at an incredibly low price, when compared with its operations in the other two regions.

The mining operations of Vale are extremely diverse, giving the company much more stability when threatened by changes in the world markets. As a world leader in iron ore, the company produces 250 million tons of iron ore and pellets, a remarkable feat considering the company's production of 90 million tons in the mid-1990s. By 2012, iron ore production for the company is expected to increase to 450 million metric tons per year.

The business aspect of manganese and alloy production was incorporated into Vale in 1999, with the company becoming the second largest manganese producer in the world, through its production of 2.3 million tons of manganese ore and 500,000 tons of manganese alloys.

Vale is the top producer of nickel on the planet with a production of 250,600 tons. A total of 63 percent of the nickel mined by Vale is meant for the production of stainless steel. By 2012, the amount of nickel processed by Vale is expected to be 500,000 metric tons.

Copper production for Vale is relatively new, only starting up in 2004 with the Sossego Mine, however that mine is averaging 140,000 tons per year. Coal is another prominent aspect of Vale, who has offices, ore search works and development of new coal businesses proposals in Venezuela, Australia, South Africa, Mozambique and Angola. In addition, Vale has minority holdings in the Chinese coal producers Longyu and Shandong Yankuang International Coking Company. The company's Moatize project in Mozambique should produce 14 million tons of metallurgic and energetic coal over 70 years.

Potash is produced by Vale at the Taquari-Vassouras Operational Unit, which is an underground mine that has a treatment plant on the surface. This is the only manufacturer of potassium chloride in Brazil and it serves as a very important component of fertilizers.

Vale also produces a white aluminum silicate that is used as a coating agent in paper, ceramics and pharmaceuticals, called Kaolin. This mineral is abundant in nature, but commercial reserves are only found in Brazil, the United Kingdom and the United States. In 2006, Vale shipped out 1.3 billion tons of the mineral.

Aluminum is a major component of the business sector of Vale, which includes bauxite mining and alumina refining and production. Vale focuses on the upstream of the production chain by developing bauxite at a low cost, In addition as alumina projects.

Vale also has an extensive investment in railroads, which is not surprising considering the significant amount of transportation that is required in the movement of their minerals, especially iron ore. From 2000 to 2006, Vale invested $1.3 billion to purchase 361 locomotives and 14,090 freight cars, with some of the locomotives being purchased for refurbishment. Only 55 of the locomotives that were bought were new ones, with each one costing $2 million. This purchase brought Vale's portfolio of railroads to 800 locomotives and 35,000 freight cars.

Some of the railroads that operate under Vale include the Vitoria a Minas railroad, which Vale has a 30 year contract on. This railroad allows Vale to transport iron from the Minas Gerais to Tubarao Port in Espirito Santa. In addition, the railroad carried 1.1 million passengers in 2006. The Carajas railroad will be owned by Vale until 2027, which Vale uses to link the iron ore mines in Para to Ponta Madeira in Maranhao.

Vale also owns the Ferraovia Centro-Atlantica railroad, which is 7,000 kilometers long and runs through six Brazilian states. The concession on this railroad will expire in 2026.

Vale owns three ports in Brazil, the Tubarao, Ponta Madeira and Sepetiba ports. In total, these three ports ship 210 million metric tons of metric ore per year.

There are also two port terminals in the state of Sergipe and two more in Espirito Santa.

Vale has produced power that it uses in its production of minerals. Whatever comes out as surplus energy, Vale sells within the market. In 2005, Vale consumed 16.9

Terawatts of power. In addition, Vale has participated in eight hydroelectric dams for a total investment of $880 million. Vale also has hydro plants in Canada and two in Indonesia, with a third in the process of being built.

In the third quarter of 2007, the company had steady earnings and a strong growth, with gross revenues coming in at $8.12 billion, the highest they have ever had for a third quarter and 9.9 percent higher than the third quarter of 2006. Profits were also up for the first three quarters of 2007 over 2006 by nearly $10 billion.

Company News

In December, the company launched a $50 million corporate-branding campaign to help consumers know about the minerals it mines and the process that takes minerals and turns them into items they use everyday. As a result, the company wants to simply be known as Vale, while spreading the message that it is proud to be Brazilian.

Also in December of 2007, Vale lost an appeal in an antitrust ruling that ordered it to get rid of certain assets to cut its influence over domestic prices. The decision came out in a three-to-two vote of Brazil's Supreme Court, which ordered Vale to sell its Ferteco mine or give up the right for first refusal on exports from Casa de Pedra iron-ore mine.

Company Trivia

With iron being a product that is used all over the planet, it has allowed Brazil to become a leading exporter of iron ore. Since Vale produces 60 percent of the iron ore in Brazil, it equates into the company producing 15 percent of all the iron ore used on the planet.

The company's investment budget of $11 billion for 2008 is the largest annual investment budget ever taken by a mining company worldwide.

Gerdau S.A. (GGB)

The largest producer of long steel in the North and South America is Gerdau S.A. The company produces and sells crude steel related to long rolled products, drawn products and long specialty products. In addition, the company offers billets, rebar, merchant bars, wire rod, drawn products and nails.

Currently, the Gerdau Group is the 14th largest steelmaker in the world, with 272 industrial and commercial facilities, five joint ventures and two associated companies. The company currently has a capacity of 23.2 million metric tons of steel per year. The company currently has 31,563 employees.

The company is based out of Porto Alegre, Brazil and has facilities, offices and factories in Brazil, Argentina, Chile, Colombia, Peru, Uruguay, Mexico, Dominican Republic, Venezuela, the United States, Canada, Spain and India.

History of Company

The company was founded by German immigrant Johann Heinrich Kasper Gerdau. After immigrating to Brazil from Hamburg, Germany in 1869, Gerdau began working as a trader and merchant, before founding a store in Cachoeira do Sul in Rio Grande do Sul.

It was around 1900 when Gerdau, moved to Porto Alegre and began a new business by buying a nail factory in 1901 and calling it Pontas de Paris.

Gerdau was aided greatly when World War II broke out and a shortage of raw materials led Gerdau into steel production, which ensured the nail operation's supply.

In 1999, Gerdau S.A. bought Ameristeel by becoming the majority shareholder, changing the name to Gerdau Ameristeel. This would be the first acquisition for Gerdau in the United States.

Profile

The core business of Gerdau is transforming scrap and iron ore into steel products, which it then sells to its clients in the civil construction, industrial and agricultural sectors in countries around the world including the United States, Argentina, Brazil, Canada, Chile, Colombia, and Peru.

Primarily, the operations are based on the integral regional market mill concept, which means raw materials are brought in by suppliers in the area, and products are then sold in that same region. The company operates in three distinct processes: minimills, integrated mills and direct reduced iron plant.

In addition, the company owns 44 fabrication shops and 26 mills in Argentina, Canada, Chile, Colombia, Peru, the United States and Uruguay, In addition as a 40 percent stake in Sidenor, a Spanish company.

It owns 44 fabrication shops and 26 mills. It also has facilities in Argentina, Canada, Chile, Colombia, Peru, the United States and Uruguay. It also holds 40% stake in the Spanish company Sidenor.

The company operates a hydroelectric

> **Gerdau is the largest producer of nails in the world.**

plant with a capacity of 125 megawatts in Rio Grande do Sul in Brazil.

The Gerdau Acos Especiais Piratini is the specialty steel business unit of Gerdau, producing engineering steels, stainless steels and tool steels for application that demand materials with a certain chemical composition.

Essentially, Gerdau's activities are divided into five business operations, Long Steel Brazil, Specialty Steel in Brazil and Spain, Acominas in Brazil, South America in Argentina, Chile, Colombia, Peru and Uruguay and North America in Canada and the United States.

In October of 2007, Gerdau, through Gerdau Ameristeel, bought Enco, which is based out of Tennessee, Arkansas, and Georgia and a producer of construction materials.

Long Steel Brazil, or Brazil Long Steel Operation, manufactured 3.8 million metric tons in 2006. During that year, the company had its steel used in the construction of the Sports Complex for the 2007 Pan-American Games, the Joao Havelange Stadium and the Olympic Village, In addition as the port terminals in Santos, Suape and Navegantes, and the expansion of the Congonhas Airport in Sao Paulo. The steel manufactured by Long Steel Brazil was also used in the construction of the National Library in Brasilia.

Specialty Steel makes auto parts, which requires strict guidelines in terms of safety and quality. The Gerdau steel is put into engines, gearboxes, steering and suspension systems of various motor vehicles.

Gerdau Acominas is used in civil construction, naval and automotive industries and in domestic appliances. In 2006, the company produced 2.9 million tons of steel. In 2006, 20 products were launched by Acominas for the wire rod market, and six for the blooms, slabs and billets market. Exports accounted for 70 percent of the volume sold by Acominas, with most of it going to Asia.

In South America, Gerdau produced 1.2 million metric tons of steel in 2006, with most of it being used for construction works like the TransMilenio project, which was a system of bus corridors built in Bogotá.

The North American division, called Gerdau Ameristeel, produced 6.8 million metric tons of steel in 2006, developing a variety of products that were used in the manufacture of #18 Jumbo anchor bolts. During 2006, the company launched Zbar, which is a type of solution used in steel for bridges and other buildings that is exposed to harsh weather on a regular basis. The company produced products that were used in hospitals, buildings, water treatment stations and bridges across North America.

Company News

For the past five years, the company has increased dividends by 778 percent, second only to Petrobras, which increased 1,248 percent in that same timeframe.

In March of 2007, they bought Mexico's Siderurgia Tultitlan for $259 billion, and they purchased the U.S. steel company Chaparral for $4.2 billion.

In June of 2007, it was announced that Terry Sutter, who had been the first choice to serve as president of Washington State University, had chosen instead to take the job of vice president and CEO of Gerdau Ameristeel.

During 2007, Gerdau Ameristeel slashed its shipments of pollutants for disposal. Originally, the company office in Waterloo had sent its pollutant byproducts, which amounted to 800 tons, to Clean Harbors in Corunna, Canada and the Waterloo Region Landfill. However, this year, the company complied with new regulations and environmental laws by diverting most of its pollutant byproduct to a Pennsylvania recycler, which removes zinc from furnace dust.

In November of 2007, the company made a major purchase in the acquisition of Quanex for $1.67 billion, which significantly increased the company's presence in the automotive industry. Quanex is the second-largest U.S. producer of special-bar quality steel. This type of steel is used in auto parts because it contains more alloys than commodity grades of steel bars. In the deal, $1.46 billion will be paid to Quanex shareholders.

Company Trivia

Within 100 years of its formation, the company's Pontas de Paris factory would become the largest nail manufacturer in the entire world.

Beams that were part of the World Trade Center were manufactured by Gerdau Ameristeel. Currently, some of those beams are on a nationwide tour before they are incorporated into a 9/11 memorial and museum, after thousands of people have signed them.

Financials

Gerdau's efforts in South America expanded greatly when the company purchased Siderperu in June 2006, which increased the company's annual output by 400,000 metric tons. In November of that year, the stake in Siderperu for Gerdaus increased to 83 percent after the company purchased 33 percent of Siderperu's equity.

In March of 2006, the company purchased assets of Callaway Building Products, which is located in Knoxville, Tennessee, while in February of 2006 they bought Fargo Iron and Metal Company out of Fargo North Dakota.

In January of 2006, the company bought 40 percent of Corporacion Sideno, which is a steel producer in Spain.

Net sales have risen every year since 2002.

.

Petrobras Energia Participaciones (PZE)

Petrobras Energia Participaciones (not to be confused with Petroleo Brasileiro, or Petrobras) is a leading oil company that uses state-of-the-art technology in the exploration, production, transportation, refining and marketing of oil and gas. It is also regularly (and confusingly) referred to as Petrobras. Although the company is based in Argentina, it has operations in Brazil, Venezuela, Peru, Ecuador, Bolivia, Colombia, and Mexico. Their refining and distribution operations are based in Argentina and Bolivia.

The company also manufactures petrochemical products, including synthetic rubber, fertilizers, styrene, and polypropylene in Brazil and Argentina. They also operate an electric utility mostly in Argentina. They also have an oil and gas trading business and own over 700 gas stations in Argentina.

They have over 5,500 oil producing wells and more than 300 gas producing wells.

History of Company

Petrobras Energia Participaciones began operations in 1946, when it was formerly known as PC Holdings S.A. It later changed its name to Perez Company S.A. in 2000, and changed its name its name once again to Petrobras Energia Participaciones S.A. in 2003.

Profile

Petrobras has three main business divisions: Refining and Distribution, Petrochemicals, and Gas and Energy.

The company's Refining and Distribution division is concentrated in Argentina and Bolivia, with the company having two refineries and 719 gas stations in Argentina. One refinery is located in San Lorenzo, and the other is in Bahia Blanca. The company also has a 28.5 percent interest in Refinor out of that country. A total of 80,800 barrels of oil are pumped out of Argentina per day, with 50,300 from the San Lorenzo Refinery, and 30,500 from the Ricardo Elitabe Refinery. The San Lorenzo Refinery has three atmospheric distillation units, two vacuum distillation units, a heavy diesel oil thermal cracking unit and an aircraft fuel production unit. All of these produce premium and regular gasoline, jet fuel, diesel fuel, fuel oil, kerosene, solvents, aromatics and asphalts.

The other refinery, Ricardo Elicabe Refinery, manufactures regular gasoline, high-grade gasoline, Podium gasoline, kerosene, diesel oil, fuel oil, asphalts and propane. In addition to the gas stations in Argentina, the company has 41 agro-centers, which meet the needs of the agriculture sector.

The company owns 28.5 percent of Refinaria del Norte. In Bolivia, the company has a 49 percent interest in Petrobras Bolivia Refinacion S.A.

The petrochemical operations of the company are performed in Argentina and Brazil, producing styrene, polystyrene, synthetic rubber, fertilizers and polypropylene.

The petrochemical operations in Brazil are done through Innova, a subsidiary of the company. Petrobras also has a 40 percent stake in Petroquimica Cuyo S.A., which is a producer and marketer of polypropylene.

The styrenics division of the company has a rubber plant in Puetro General San Martin, which has a capacity of 160,000 tons of styrene per year and 57,000 tons of synthetic rubber per year.

The company also has a polystyrene plant at Zarate, which has a production capacity of 66,000 tons of polystyrene per year and 14,000 tons of bio-oriented polystyrene per year. In addition, there is an ethylene plant in San Lorenzo, with a production capacity of 20,000 tons per year.

A fertilizer division is located at a complex in Campana, which can produce 200,000 tons per year of urea and 560,000 tons per year of liquid fertilizers.

The Gas and Energy sector of the company produces oil and gas and liquefied petroleum gas. The company is also engaged in transporting gas in Southern Argentina, along with processing and marketing of natural gas liquids.

The company is also a part of electrical generation, transmission and distribution, providing electricity generation to the Genelba Power Plant and the Pichi Picun Leufu Hydroelectric Complex.

Through Transener, Enecor S.A. and Yacylec S.A., the company engages in the electricity transmission business, and in the electric distribution business through its interest in Edesur.

The company also specializes in the exploration of oil and gas, as well as its production. Currently, there are eight production or exploration areas currently being pursued or used by Petrobras.

In the oil and gas Exploration division, the company owns 100 percent of Petrobras Energia Peru, Petrobras Energia Venezuela, Corod Produccion, Ecuadortic and Petrobras Energia Ecuador. It owns 19.2 percent in Petrolera Entre Lomas and 49 percent in both Coroil and Inversora Mata.

Company News and Trivia

Petrobras, Warner Bros. Pictures, and Village Roadshow Pictures recently announced a partnership in which Petrobras will have a product placement in a movie called Speed Racer, also known as Meteoro. The movie is based on the Japanese animation series created by Tatsuo Yoshida during the 1960's. Expected release date is in May 2008.

Petroleo Brasileiro S.A. [Petrobras] (PBR)

Petroleo Brasileiro, or Petrobras (not to be confused with Petrobras Energia Participaciones [PZE]), is a Brazilian oil company which has a significant output of two million barrels of oil per day, making it a major distributor of oil products throughout the world. The company is also a world leader in the development of technology, which can be used for ultra-deep and deep water oil drilling and production. The company has business operations in 18 countries in North America, Asia, South America, Europe and Africa.

Approximately 55.7 percent of the company's shares are owned by the Brazilian government, with other portions being traded on Bovespa.

The company is also a very large supporter of arts, culture and the environment in Brazil, including being a primary supporter of whale conservation and research through the Brazilian Humpback Whale Institute.

Operations are carried out by the company across the world, while they are headquartered in Brazil; they do business in 26 countries, including Argentina, Angola, Bolivia, Colombia, the United States and Nigeria.

The company has refineries in the United States, Argentina, as well as 14 in Brazil. The company currently has over 60,000 employees.

History of Company

After Law 2.004 was passed by Brazilian President Getulio Vargas, Petrobras was created in 1953 and allowed to incorporate to undertake oil sector activities in Brazil on behalf of the government.

Petrobras held a monopoly on the activities connected with oil exploration and production operations, In addition as all the activities related to the oil, natural gas and derivative sector from 1954 to 1997.

During this time, the company became a leader in derivative marketing in Brazil and was awarded the Offshore Technology Conference Award in 1992, which is the most important award in the sector. The company received the prestigious award again in 2001.

In 1997, thanks to Petrobras, Brazil entered the club of only 16 countries in the world that produce more than one million barrels of oil a day. It was also during this year that the monopoly on oil industry activities ended for Petrobas, when President Fernando Henrique Cardoso signed Law #9.478.

In 2003, Petrobras surpassed the two million barrel per day mark, and three years later, production at platform P-50 was started in the Campos Basin, allowing Brazil to achieve oil self-sufficiency.

The company currently ranks as the 14th largest oil company in the world, and seventh largest among all publicly-traded companies.

In 2007, the company began production on the Comperj Integration Center in Sao Goncalo, which will help the company become a pioneer in engineering and in the petrochemical area. In addition, the facility will be used to train individuals in specialized labor practices.

Also in 2007, the company started up the P-54 platform, which created 2,600 direct jobs and 10,000 indirect jobs for the country.

In September of 2007, construction work began on the Abreu e Lima Refinery in Recife, and the Piranema Platform in Sergipe, which is a refinery that will be the first to produce 100 percent heavy oil.

Profile

Petrobras operates several different divisions: exploration and production, gas and energy, transportation and storage and distribution.

In terms of Exploration and Production, Petrobras is a leader in the technology used for ultra-deep water exploration, allowing the company to find oil and produce it at favorable costs in offshore fields and very deep depths. Opening up the exploration and production area to international partners has allowed Petrobras to generate investment prospects in other parts of the world.

Petrobras goal is to increase production in the oil and gas reserves, utilizing a sustainable manner, as well as expanding operation areas that have exploration and production potential where the company can use its operating, technical and technological capabilities.

Petrobras considers natural gas to be the fuel of the future and a significant prospect for Brazil, which has an enormous pool of natural gas reserves. In addition, the company is expanding into different forms of energy, including biofuel and solar power.

Petrobras is also in the transportation and storage sector through its company Petrobras Transporte S.A., which performs the transportation of oil and gas to various domestic and foreign markets around the world. Petrobras has stated that as a transportation and storage service provider, it respects the environment, while keeping the interest of shareholders in mind at all times, as well as contributing to the development of Brazil.

Petrobras Distribuidor provides services to 7,000 gas stations across Brazil, in both cities and along highways. The company is a leader in Brazilian oil byproduct distribution, with more than 10,000 major companies as their customers.

The distribution side of Petrobras, which is Brazil's largest, specializes in automotive, maritime, railway and aviation industries, with Petrobraas Distribuidora's products used in various applications.

The company states there is a strict control system in place to ensure high quality is placed on the Brazilian market's leadership.

The company also operates several oil platforms, including several of which were set up in 2007. The latest was the Platform P-54 which started production on December 11, adding 180,000 barrels per day to their domestic production.

In November of 2007, the company added the P-52, which has the same capacity as the P-54, and the FPSCO Cidade de Vitoria, which was installed in the Espirito Santo Basin.

More than 80 percent of the oil produced by the company comes from offshore fields. Onshore oil production is currently at 230,000 barrels per day.

The company plans to add three new oil platforms and one gas platform in 2008, which will extract 460,000 barrels of oil per day and ten million cubic meters of gas per day.

Company News

In November of 2007, the company announced that it had discovered the largest oil and natural gas field in the world, just off the coast of Rio de Janeiro, which they believe has as much as eight billion barrels of oil. If it turns out successfully, it will be the largest oil discovery since Kashagan in Kazakhstan in 2000. This reserve would increase the oil reserves of Brazil by 62 percent.

In 2007, Petrobras was named by the Financial Times as one of the world's 50 largest companies for the year.

The company announced this year that it would be producing second-generation ethanol for export. The company evaluated 40 mills for production, and had five projects approved. By 2012, the company expects to produce 4.5 billion liters per day.

In November, Petrobras launched the Development and Citizenship program, which they will finance until 2012, projects to help reduce poverty, give support to children and promote professional training to the people of Brazil.

2007 was a big year for the company in terms of awards. It was granted the Latin America Deal of the Year award by Project Finance International for the Henrique Lage Refinery Modernization Project's Financial Structuring. This award is considered to be the most important in the sector.

The company also won the Best Investor Relations Program for Retail Investors Award, which is an award presented to the company that ranks high in terms of general prestige, respect to performance and investor relations.

The company also won an award at the British Magazine Petroleum Economist's Award ceremony, when they received the Investor Communications Team of Year Award due to the company's International Relations Team project. In addition, the company was also a finalist for the Best Youth Education Program Category and the Health & Safety Project of the Year, the second year in a row that the company was a finalist for these awards, which are considered significant for the industry.

Company Trivia

Petrobras owned the Petrobras 36 Oil Platform, the world's largest oil platform in the world, until it was destroyed by an explosion on March 15, 2001, which led to it sinking five days later.

In December of 2007, the company set a daily oil production record in Brazil by breaking the 2,000,000 barrel level, a level met by very few companies in the world.

<u>Ultrapar Holdings Inc. (UGP)</u>

Ultrapar Holdings, Inc., through its subsidiaries, distributes liquefied petroleum gas [LPG] in Brazil. This Sao Paulo based company distributes LPG primarily to residential and industrial customers throughout a large portion of Brazil. The company also manufactures and markets chemicals, such as ethylene oxide, ethylene glycols, and methyl-ethyl-ketone. In addition, they produce specialty chemicals used in cosmetics, detergents, textiles, foods, agricultural chemicals, and various other household and industrial products. Ultrapar Holdings also provides integrated road transportation and logistics planning services for fuel and chemicals. The company currently employs 9,500 employees. With its headquarters in Brazil, the company, through its subsidiaries, has industrial units in three Mexican cities: Guadalajara, Coatzacoalcos and San Juan del River, and they have one additional unit in Venezuela.

History of Company

In the early 1930s, Ernesto Igel created the Companhia de Gas a Domicilio, which became Ultragaz. The company started out with three trucks and 166 customers, however with the outbreak of World War II, and the United States gas supply disruption, the company began importing gas from Argentina.

By 1970, Ultrapar moved into the Brazilian petrochemical industry, through the creation of Oxiteno S.A. The plant was built in Maua and became a leading producer of ethylene oxide and its by-products in Brazil.

Later, Ultrapar expanded its petrochemical and distribution business through its acquisitions and capacity expansions. At that time, Ultrapar started to focus on three business lines, LPG distribution, the manufacture of chemicals and petrochemicals and the storage and transportation of chemicals. In 1997, Ultrapar started the Ultrasystem, building a new LPG bottling plant and expanding the Oxiteno plant, located in the Petrochemical Comoplex of Camacari.

In October 1999, Ultrapar's shares began trading on the Bovespa and New York Stock Exchanges. Three years later, the company restructured with Gipoia Ltd merging into Ultrapar and Oxiteno into Ultrapar, with Ultrapar owning 100 percent of both Oxiteno and Ultragaz.

In 2003, Ultrapar aquired Royal Dutch/Shell N.V. in Brazil, as well as the Mexican specialty chemicals company, Berci Group.

Profile

One of the most successful operations in Brazil is Ultrapar, which has operations in Brazil, Mexico, Argentina and the United States. The company is a distributor of fuels through Ultragaz and Ipiranga, a producer of chemicals though Oxiteno and operates integrated logistics solutions through Ultracargo.

Ultrapar is a LPG distribution leader in Brazil, with a 24 percent of the market, supplying approximately 10 million homes throughout Brazil, as well as to 30,000 companies. It is also one of the ten largest independent distributors in the entire world.

Oxiteno is the largest producer of ethylene oxide in South America and a foremost manufacturer of specialty chemicals. Their products are used in cosmetics, detergents, paints, PET packaging, textiles, agro-chemicals and other consumer and industrial markets. They have five manufacturing plants in Brazil and two in Mexico with their products exported to 40 countries on five continents.

In 2006, Ultracargo celebrated its 40th birthday and the fact that it is one of the largest providers of logistic services in Brazil. The company utilizes several terminals, railroads, highways and coastal shipping, which are strategically located in Brazil's main ports and petrochemical centers.

Currently, the company is listed on the ISE index, which is a corporate sustainability index on the Bovespa stock exchange, which is comprised of stocks issued by companies who have shown a commitment to sustainable practices and social responsibility.

Ultrapar recently expanded its oil based distribution business through the acquisition of Ipiranga Group, expanding its reach to the South and Southeast regions of Brazil, allowing the company to become Brazil's second largest distributor of fuels and lubricants, achieving a market share of 15 percent.

Company News

In September of 2007, Forbes magazine stated there were rumors circulating that Ultrapar was showing a great deal of interest in acquiring Exxon's Brazil assets.

Brazil Financial Stocks

Banco Bradesco (BBD)

Banco Bradesco provides banking and financial services to individuals and companies serving customers all over the world. Their branch and service network is the largest in Brazil. They are also the largest insurance, pension and titulos de capitalizacao provider in Brazil, based on insurance premiums, pensions plan contributions and savings plan income. Their headquarters is located in Osasco. Banco Bradesco has been in existence for over 60 years and is considered the country's leader in lending with $61.3 billion in revenue in 2007.

History of Company

The company was founded in the city of Marilia in 1943, under the name Banco Brasileiro de Descontos. Their initial customers were small retailers, government workers and landowners. Other banks pursued larger landowners and businesses.

In 1946, the company moved its headquarters to Sao Paulo. By 1951, the company had become the largest private-sector bank in Brazil. In 1953, the company established its headquarters in Osasco. In 1956, the Bradesco Foundation was created to help provide free education for poor children, teenagers and adults. In 1968, the company began offering its first Bradesco Credit Card.

Banco Bradesco was the first Latin American company to buy a computer

By the 1970s, they began to expand into areas of lending and the financing of vehicles. That same decade,

Bradesco opened 17 more bank branches, and in 1978 reached the 1,000 branch milestone. In the 1980s, they began utilizing automated teller machines and debit cards which were used throughout Latin America. In 2000, Banco Bradesco began operations in Buenos Aires, and established securities operations in New York that year.

Profile

Considered to be one of the big four banks of Brazil, the company has nearly 3,000 branches across the country and offers services which include insurance, pension plans, annuities, Internet banking, credit card services and free Internet access for customers. In addition to its branches in Brazil, the company has branches in New York, Grand Cayman and Nassau, along with subsidiaries in Nassau, Luxembourg, Buenos Aires, Grand Cayman and Tokyo.

The company has two separate divisions: the banking group and the pension, insurance and savings group. As of 2006, the company had 14.2 million insurance policyholders, 16.8 million checking accounts, 35.2 million savings accounts, and 2.3 million certified saving plans. Over 1,200 Brazilian and multinational companies are corporate customers of the bank, and the bank processes over 12.4 million daily transaction, with 10 million occurring through ATMs and 2.4 million in their 3,008 branches.

Altogether, the company also has 24,099 ATMs and 2,542 special banking posts utilized by corporate clients.

Their banking services include checking and savings accounts, consumer lending, housing loans and agricultural loans. They also offer debit card services, payment processing, and capital markets services.

They provide easy-checking accounts that are a combination of checking and savings accounts and provide personal loans to customers, consisting primarily of short-term loans, with an average of a five percent rate of interest.

As of 2006, the company had 29,860 real estate loans outstanding, which had been granted by the Sistema Financeiro Habitacional or Carteria Hipotecaria Habitacional, at interest rates of eight to 16 percent over five to 20 years.

The bank also offers Visa, American Express and MasterCard credit cards to their customers. The company offers electronic solutions for receipt and payment management for paying credit cards and bills.

A wide variety of services are provided to corporate clients, which include employee checking accounts, salary cards for employees, company credit cards. The bank also offers trading in stocks, bonds, futures, options, and Brazilian government securities.

The insurance, pension and certified savings division of the company operates through their division, Grupo Bradesco de Seguros e Previdencia. They provide health, life, accident, auto, property and casualty insurance. In total, there are 2.6 million health and dental policyholders. 12,000 companies work with the bank as part of the health insurance network, which includes 9,500 specialized clinics, 9,000 laboratories, 14,400 physicians, 3,000 hospitals, 1,200 clinics and 5,500 dentists. In 2006, the company insured 9.3 customers with life and accident insurance. 1.3 million customers are covered by the automobile insurance policies provided by the bank. The organization utilizes a network of over 30,000 insurance brokers. Over 2.3 million clients participate in the bank's pension plan.

Company News

On January 26, 2008, Bradesco was in negotiations to acquire a majority stake in Agora, the largest brokerage firm in Brazil.

Due to the Brazilian economy, Bradesco was featured on Cramer's Mad Money financial show on October 30, 2007, with Banco Bradesco being called the best way to play the Brazilian utopia. Reasons given were that it had few bad loans, was a market leader in insurance and pension plans, and had 20 percent of the ATMs in a increasingly wealthy country.

Company Trivia

Banco Bradesco was the first company in Latin America to acquire a computer, which they purchased in 1962.

Banco Itau Holding Financeira S.A. (ITU)

Banco Itau Holding Financeria is a bank holding company headquartered out of Sao Paulo, which provides retail and corporate banking services, and accounts for 11 percent of all retail banking services in Brazil, making it the second largest bank in that country. The company has 50,000 employees. The company also owns Investimentos Itau, which is a large investment company.

History of Company

Banco Itau was founded in 1945 with the name Banco Central de Credito. In 1964, the company merged with Banco Federal de Credito and Banco Itau, before acquiring Banco Sul Americano and Banco da America in 1966 and 1969.

In the 1970's, Banco Italu merged with Banco Alianca, Banco Portugues do Brasil and Banco Uniao Comercial, as well as opening branches in New York and Buenos Aires.

In 1985, Banco Itau acquired Banco Pinto de Magalhaes, expanding during a time when most Brazilian banks were contracting. In 1995, the bank acquired Banco Frances e Brasileiro, as well as Banerj in 1997, BEMGE in 1998, Banestado in 2000 and BEG in 2001.

The company invested heavily in automation in the 1990's, through the establishment of ATMs, while reducing staff by more than 50 percent.

In 1994, the company continued to expand by creating Banco Itau Europa, Itau Argentina and Itau Bank. In 1997, the company bought Bamerindus Luxembourg, and Banco Del Buen Ayre in 1998.

The bank formed alliances with other banks in the late 1990's, including Bankers Trust in 1996, Banco BPI in Portugal, Banco Itau in 2002 and Banco Itau-BBA in 2003, causing it to become the largest wholesale bank in Brazil. In 2002, the company bought Banco Fiat for its auto financing, then bought BankBoston in 2006, allowing the company to increase its clients by 300,000 and expanding its assets by R$22 billion.

Profile

The Banco Itau Holding Financeira has three primary operations, including banking through Banco Itau S.A., corporate banking through Banco Itau BBA, and consumer credit to non-account customers through Itaucred.

Banco Itau S.A. provides a variety of services to its customers, including small business banking, retail banking, credit cards, asset management, and brokerage products. Itau Holding had 12.9 million customers at the end of 2006. Itau Personnalite is the division of the company that offers services to high-income individuals. In total, there are 159 branches in the major Brazilian cities.

With over 6,400 accounts, the Itau Private bank is one of the largest banks in the country, with 218 units located across Brazil. The subsidiary, Itau Empresas maintains the day-to-day operations for 34,500 middle-market corporate customers, providing collection services and payment services. The company also offers a great deal of other financial services, including investments, insurance and credit products. The credit products offer capital loans, inventory financing, equipment leasing, and letters of credit. In 2006, the company had 13.4 million MasterCard and Visa credit cards in circulation, representing 17 percent of the Brazilian credit card market. Also, the company provides security services in capital markets, where it acts as the transfer agent.

Itau Corretora de Valores offers brokerage services on the Sao Paulo Stock Exchange and Brazilian Futures and Commodities Market. It also has brokerage operations in New York, London and Hong Kong.

Itau Holding operates an insurance business in Brazil, with the company having a 27.5 percent equity interest in AGF Brasil Seguros. The company offers insurance in life (67% of the market), auto (15%), and property and casualty (7%).

Banco Itau BBA operates in the corporate and investment banking market to 1,100 corporate customers. In 2006, the company entered into an agreement with Bank of America Corporation to obtain the rights to negotiate the acquisition of BAC operations in Brazil, Chile and Uruguay. The company has 178,000 active customers through its subsidiaries, Banco Itau Europa and Banco Itau Europa Luxembourg, which provide offshore private banking business to Brazilian clientele.

Itaucred consists of transactions for non-account holders, through its own internal operations and its partnerships with Companhia Brasileira de Distribuicao and Lasa, Banco Fiat and Banco Intercap. The company consists of three components, automobile financing, credit cards and offering credit to low-income individuals. In terms of financing automobiles, the company had approximately 1.7 million contracts in 2006, 72 percent of which were non-account holding customer contracts. The company provides leases through 14,000 dealers. The low-income ventures are operated through Financeira Americanas Ita and Financeira Ita.

Company News

On January 22, the company announced that its M&A business grew by $7.5 billion, or 12.6 percent from 2006. This made it among the top 10 financial advisors in Latin America, ranking at eighth place, above even Merrill Lynch.

In early 2008, Banco announced it would be selling a 15 percent stake in the Brazilian credit card company Redecard through a share offering, amounting to nearly $1.4 billion.

Uniao de Bancos Brasileiros S.A. [Unibanco] (UBB)

The third-largest bank in Brazil, Uniao de Bancos Brasileiros S.A., also known as Unibanco and often called Brazilian Banks Union, has been existence for over 75 years, with its headquarters out of Sao Paulo. The bank experienced significant growth after their purchase of Banco Nacional in 1995, which had previously gone bankrupt in the early 1990's.

The bank provides various financial services to its customers, including consumer credit, checking accounts, loans, insurance, pensions, investment funds and brokerage services.

The bank owns several other companies, including Fininvest, Hipercard, Luizacred, Pontocred, Banco Dibens and Unicard.

History

Unibanco was founded in September 27, 1924, when a small-town merchant, Joao Moreira Salles, set up a banking department in his store. Founded as Casa Moreira Salles of Pocos de Caldas in Minas Gerais, the bank eventually became the third-largest in Brazil.

By 1931, the banking section had grown so large that it was converted into an independent financial institution. In 1940, Banco Moreira Salles was formed when Casa Bancaria Moreira Salles, Banco Machadense and Casa Bancaria de Botelhos was merged into one company. The company then opened its first branch outside of Minas Gerais in 1941, with a branch in Rio de Janeiro, and subsequently by another branch in Sao Paulo the next year. By 1945, the bank had 34 branches throughout Brazil, increasing to 63 in 1950, and 191 in 1964.

Over the next twenty years, the bank grew through mergers and acquisitions, including the Deltec, Light & Power Company and the Azevedo Antunes Group in 1966 to create Banco de Investimento do Brasil. In 1968, it partnered with Commerzbank AG, then with Credit Suisse in 1969, Dai-Ichi Kangyo Bank in 1972 and Philadelphia International Investment Corporation in 1973.

One significant merger for the company took place in 1967, when it merged with Banco Agricola Mercantil to create Uniao de Bancos Brasileiros. The new company had 8,570 employees, 333 branches and one million accounts around Brazil. At that time, it would be the largest bank branch network in the country, and was the second largest private bank in Brazil. In 1975, the conglomeration of banks and financial institutions went under the name Unibanco.

In 1983, the bank opened three 24 hour service centers for the public, allowing customers to make deposits and withdrawals anytime day or night. Eight years later, the bank created the 24 hour bank by phone service, making it one of the pioneers in the area of telephone banking.

In 1991, the bank founded the Instituto Moreira Salles, which was designed to promote culture programming for the public. Also during the 1990's, the bank achieved a customer base of 18 million, primarily due to the Data Processing Center that opened in 1993, which allowed the bank to increase its operation processing capacity by 40 percent.

Additional acquisitions would follow for the bank in the 1990's, and by 2000, it would have 1,623 branches

Profile

Unibanco is a full service financial institution, providing banking products and services for both individuals and corporations. The company is divided into four divisions: Retail, Wholesale, Insurance and Pension Plans, and Wealth Management.

The retail business of the company provides services that include Internet and telephone banking, personal banking services, corporate banking and credit card services. Currently, the company has 30 million credit cards issued. One of their primary cards is the Hipercard, which is the official card of Wal-Mart in Brazil, with over 6.5 million of cards issued. Unibanco also provides ATMs, personal computer banking and fund transfers available to their individual customers.

As of 2006, there were 18,000 banking sites for the bank across Brazil, consisting of 940 retail branches, 316 corporate-site branches, 714 Fininvest stores, kiosks and mini-stores, 12,000 Fininvest retailers, 341 LuizaCred retailers, 378 PontoCred retailers and 3,201 24 Hour branches.

The wholesale part of the business involves corporate lending, capital markets, trade finance and investment. This is done through 400 institutional investors and 2,150 economic groups. The company is also in the business of corporate lending and structured finance products.

Unibanco also provides financing through import and exporting services to corporate customers, through funding it receives from correspondent banks. The company's brokerages provide equity and debt securities and trading services to be used on Brazilian exchanges. It also researches 80 listed companies for clients worldwide.

The insurance and pension plan sector of Unibanco provides life, auto, health, property, casualty and extended warranty insurance through UASEG, a joint venture with the American International Group. Unibanco owns over half of the voting shares of UASEG.

Unibanco utilizes 12,600 brokers, call centers and website to market its insurance products and services. There are 1,300 corporate customers and 800 individual customers.

The final division for the company is wealth management, which is operated through Unibanco Asset Management and its Private Bank. This division provides income and equity mutual funds to customers and provides portfolio management for corporations, pension funds and banking clients. Unibanco has five offices dedicated to this division, in Sao Paulo, Rio de Janeiro, Porto Alegre, Ribeirao Preto and Belo Horizonte, and a total of 8,500 customers.

Company News

In January, the company sold a 15 percent stake in Redecard, which is a Brazilian credit card company. The 15 percent stake was a joint holding with Banco Itau.

In 2007, the company saw its loan growth rise by nearly 30 percent, exceeding company expectations.

Company Trivia

Unibanco is still controlled by the founding Moreira Salles family, even after 80 years. Up until recently, the family business was headed by Walter Moreira Salles, who had also served as Brazilian ambassador to Britain and Finance Minister. His son, Pedro Moreira Salles is now the CEO of the company.

Gafisa S.A. (GFA)

One of the largest builders in Brazil, Grafisa has seen two name changes in its history, and created a vast range of building and construction enterprises across the country. 90 percent of its business takes place in Sao Paulo and Rio de Janeiro. Currently, the company has two major shareholders, which include Equity International and GP Investments.

History of Company

Founded in 1954, Gafisa has become one of the largest builders in Brazil. Initially based in Rio de Janeiro, the company began its operations under the name Gomes de Almeida. Later, in 1984, the company changed its name to Gafisa Imobiliaria. In 1997, GP Investimentos began an association with Gafisa Imobiliaria, at which time the name of the company was changed to Gafisa S.A., when it became a publicly traded company. In 2003, GP Investimentos became the majority shareholder with 60 percent of the shares.

Since its inception, the company has constructed over 900 buildings including apartments, commercial buildings, luxury condos, and shopping centers.

In 2004, the company expanded operations with the creation of the New Business Board of Directors, which focuses on urban subdivision construction, with the goal of building in markets outside of Rio de Janeiro and Sao Paulo.

Also in 2004, the company went into partnership with Equity International Properties, a real estate company out of North America that invests in Latin America. EIP invested in Gafisa, with control of 32 percent of its shares.

Profile

The primary business of the company is construction of residential buildings. However, they also build commercial projects. In 2006, middle to upper-income residential developments amounted to 65 percent of its operations. However, the company also engages in the development of land subdivisions and low-income housing.

In addition to doing their own construction services, it also contracts it out to third parties, which allows them to operate in 35 markets including Sao Paulo, Rio de Janeiro, Belem, Fortaleza, Natal, Curitiba, Belo Horizonte, Manaus, Porto Alegre and Salvador.

In an effort to expand its construction business, Gafisa purchased 60 percent of Alphaville Urbanismo, a residential community development company in Brazil that develops and markets residential communities in metropolitan areas, to go after the upper income and upper-middle income families. They also began a project developing, constructing and managing low-income residential products of 1,000 or more units.

Gafisa also sells residential units, residential communities and commercial buildings, through its brokerage subsidiary, Gafisa Vendas. Gafisa sells middle and upper-income, which usually have three to four bedrooms, with three parking spaces. Gafisa also sells lower-income housing units, with the building units consisting of two to three bedrooms.

Three of the commercial buildings that Gafisa built are the Sunplaza Personal Office in Rio de Janeiro, the Icarai Corporate and the Gafisa Corporate and Eldorado Business Tower in Sao Paulo.

Construction services are often contracted out by Gafisa, helping third parties build residential and commercial projects in Brazil. Recently, the company has won 30 percent of the bids it has bid on.

Company News

On December 11, the company stock price hit a new high after spiking by $3.15 to $42.56.

Company Trivia

If you added up all the residential and commercial space that Gafisa has built in Rio de Janeiro and Sao Paulo, it would total nine million square meters.

Past Financials of Company

In the third quarter of 2007, Gafisa saw its earnings gain 12 percent due to the lower borrowing costs and a higher demand for homes in Brazil. Their net income rose by more than 10%.

Brazil Telecom Stocks

Brasil Telecom Participacoes S.A. (BRP)

Brasil Telecom Participacoes (BRP), not to be confused with Brasil Telecom (BTM), is based in Brasilia, Brazil, and is a holding company that operates landline telephone services throughout Brazil. They also provide public telephones, supplemental local services, intraregional, interregional and international long-distance services, networking services, and wireless services.

Company History

The company was established in 1998 and was formerly known as Tele Centro Sul Participacoes S.A. It then changed its name to Brasil Telecom Participacoes S.A. in 2000. The company is considered to be a subsidiary of Solpart Participacoes S.A.

Profile

The company provides telecommunication services, and has 8.4 million lines of service throughout the region. The company owns over 277,000 public telephones. They also provide an assortment of local services that include call forwarding, voice mail and caller ID.

Long-distance services are provided throughout Brazil and internationally. The company also provides fixed-to-mobile services which carries calls that begin on a fixed-line telephone and end on a mobile phone. The company entered into an agreement with Telemar Norte Leste and Telecomunicacoes de Sao Paulo to provide international services.

Network services provided include data transmission services that are offered to residential and corporate clients with a service called Turbo, a high-speed Internet system that runs on the ADSL technology. They also provides other data transmission services for corporate and government customers.

The data transmission services consist of point-to-point networks, which is for corporate customers, network infrastructure networks for corporate security, Internet access networks, which is for corporate customers and advanced services networks, which is a blend of several technologies and services.

The Internet services include broadband Internet through BrTurbo, its ISP, as well as iG, which generates revenue from advertising and e-commerce services. The company has a client base in excess of 300,000. The service includes blogs, chatting, and photo albums. Recently, iG entered into an agreement with the Internet game, Second Life, which will allow the company to provide products to mobile users, including ring tones, cards, images and more.

Currently, the company is part of the Fixed Mobile Convergence Alliance, a 22 member association that provides products and technologies to clients of all the members. The company competitors include Embratel, Intelig, Global Village Telecom, Telesp, Telemar, Companhia de Telecomnicacoes do Brasil Central, Sercomtel Teelcomunicacoes, TIM, Claro and Vivo.

Brasil Telecom S.A. (BTM)

Brasil Telecom, not to be confused with Brasil Telecom Participacoes (BRP), is headquartered out of Brasilia. It is one of only three land-line companies in Brazil since the break-up of Telebras. The company was originally called Tele Centro Sul, and its service covers Acre, Goias, Mato Grosso, Mato Grosso do Sul, Parana, Rondonia, Santa Catarina, Rio Grande do Sul Tocantins, and the Brazilian Federal District. The company has over 16,000 employees.

History of Company

The company began in 1963 as Telecomunicacoes do Parana S.A.-Telepar. It later changed its name to Brasil Telecom S.A. in 2000. Brasil Telecom S.A. is a subsidiary of Brasil Telecom Participacoes S.A.

Profile

Brasil Telecom provides numerous services to its subscribers, including local services, installation, monthly subscriptions, public telephones, supplemented local services, long-distance services within Brazil, intrastate services, international long-distance, Internet, data transmission and wireless services.

They own public telephones and they provide fixed-to-mobile services, voice mail, call waiting, call forwarding and called ID services.

For international services, the company allows calls to any region within Brazil, as well as outside the country. The company has agreements with Telemar Norte Leste and Telecommunicacoes de Sao Paulo to provide these services

The company has a service that consists of interconnection network services, and lease of facilities. The company provides Data Transmission Services through various access points. The company offers a service called Turbo, which is a broadband, ADSL service for high speed Internet for both residential and corporate customers. They also generate revenue through advertising, e-commerce, traffic generation and broadband access.

The client base for broadband is about 300,000, with paid services base amounting to 200,000. The company, which uses the service through iG, has launched several tools online, including blogs.

Company News

On January 17, it was announced that Alcatel-Lucent, won a contract to operate and maintain the telecom networks of Brasil Telecom. This two year contract amounts to $1.1 billion.

In late-2007, Tele Norte Leste Participacoes, which has the Oi brand, announced it was in discussions to purchase Brasil Telecom. The cost of the deal is approximately $2.7 billion.

Net Servicos de Comunicacoe (NETC)

The largest cable television provider in Latin America, Net Servicos de Comunicacao has more than 1.9 million subscribers. In addition to cable television services, the company provides broadband Internet services to 830,000 subscribers, as well as telephone over cable under the Net Fone via Embratel name, with 257,000 subscribers. The company trades on the New York Stock Exchange and Bovespa Stock Exchange.

Company History

Formed in 1991, the company came into existence due to an acquisition of several small cable TV companies in several locations. The first acquired company was located in the state of Mato Grosso do Sul, which only had 100 subscribers at the time. Between 1991 and 1993, seven more companies were acquired, six in the Sao Paulo State, and one in the state of Goais, ending up with 2,000 subscribers.

As business continued to increase, the company added two partners, Globopar in 1993 and Ralph Partners II in 1994. They each had a one third ownership.

Between 1996 and 1998, the cable network grew, through the purchase of several companies, including Net Belo Horizonte, Net Anapolis and Net Piracicaba, to become the largest multi-subscriber operator for televisiion in the country.

In 2000, the company purchased VICOM, a national company with 3,000 stations that were used for satellite telecommunications. That same year, the company bought Net Sul, which was the second largest cable operator in Brazil with 374,100 subscribers.

The company changed its name to Net Servicos de Comunicacao in 2002.

Profile

The company is a provider of pay-television and Internet access to 1.8 million homes in 44 cities of Brazil. They offer high-speed Internet through its NET Virtua service to over 725,000 subscribers, in addition to voice services through NET Fone via Embratel, which has over 180,000 subscribers.

In 2006, the company started working with Embratel, to begin the process of integrating Voice over IP technology to allow subscribers to make local, long-distance and international calls from any telephone, charging by the minute.

The company's primary business is in the pay-television service, which includes cable and pay-per-view. They provide this service in several cities in Brazil, including Sao Paulo, Rio de Janeiro, Belo Horizonte, Porto Alegre, Recife, Brasilia, Goiania, Curitiba and Florianopolis.

This service is provided in three packages, digital, premium, and advanced, with digital service only available to customers in Rio de Janeiro, Sao Paulo and Porto Alegre. The digital cable service provides high quality broadcasting and video-on-demand [VOD] services.

The pay-per-view services include broadcasting sporting events and musical concerts and the company has exclusive broadcast rights to broadcast Brazilian Soccer Championships and various state soccer championships. Three percent of total revenues of the company come from pay-per-view.

Broadband services are available in 12 Brazilian cities including Sao Paulo, Rio de Janeiro, Brasilia, Belo Horizonte, Santos, Sorocaba, Curitaba, Porto Alegre,

Campinas, Florianopolis, Campo Grande and Goiania, reaching 3 million homes and over 725,000 residential subscribers.

The voice services are provided to over 180,000 customers in Sao Paulo, Campinas, Santos, Rio de Janeiro, Porto Alegre, Curitiba, Florianopolis, Belo Horizonte and Brasilia.

Company News

In March of 2007, the company announced that Joao Adalberto Elek would be the new Chief Financial Officer and Director of Investor Relations of the Company.

In November of 2007, the company launched a line of NET products in cities serviced by Vivax.

In late 2007, the company was downgraded by S&P Equity Research from Buy to Hold due to rising expenses and increased competition from satellite television.

Tele Norte Celular Participacoes S.A. (TCN)

Tele Norte Celular Participacoes is a telecommunications company that serves Para, Amazonas, Maranhao, Amapa and Roraima in the north part of Brazil. Currently, the company provides services through Time Division Multiple Access [TDMA] technology, and its analog service runs on Advanced Mobile Phone Service [AMPS] technology.

The company has a series of prepaid and contract customers, in addition to corporate customers.

Company History

Another relatively new company, Tele Norte was established on February 28, 1998 while the Brazilian government was going through the process of deregulating the telecommunications industry.

Profile

The company provides services, which include caller ID, voicemail, fax services, e-mail access, and bank statement access. Also, the company provides mobile services to subscribers of other service providers in Tele Norte's area. Tele Norte now has over 1.2 million subscribers.

They provide their services in the form of contracts that use rate plans, and prepaid cards with 22.7 percent of its service revenues coming from monthly subscription plan customers.

An Internet service is provided by the company called i.amazoniacelular, which includes communication, news, remote access to personal computers and other Internet services.

They also sell handsets, accessories, calling cards and provides activation services through four distribution channels, a network of independent local distributors, company-owned stores, a direct sales force, and prepaid cards at 16,000 point-of-sale locations.

The company has a monthly billing system for its subscription customers utilizing six billing cycles in a month to make billing and collection run more efficiently. It also developed a fraud management system which monitors calling patterns.

Company News

In 2007, Oi, also known as Telemar, bought a controlling interest in Tele Norte. The company bought 51.86 percent of the company's common shares and .09 percent of its preferred. The purchase was done so that Oi could expand its coverage in Amazonas, Para, Amapa, Roraima and Maranhao.

Telecomunicacoes de Sao Paulo (TSP)

Telecommunicacoes de Sao Paulo, also known as Telesp, is a communications company that operates in the Sao Paulo State in Brazil, providing fixed line telephone services. The company trades on the New York Stock Exchange, with its headquarters based out of Sao Paulo, Brazil.

The company generates revenue in excess of $8 billion annualy. The parent company for Telesp is Telefonica.

Company History

The history of Telesp begins in 1998, when the state-owned telecom monopoly ended, which resulted in Telebras, of which Telesp was a part of, was being privatized. Telefonica took over Telesp and the company was renamed Telefonica, however the corporate name is still in use.

In March of 2006, the company, along with Telefonica Data Brasil Holding and Telefonica Empresas, restructured the parent Telefonica's multimedia connection services and data transmission services. This led to a merger of Telefonica Data Brasil Holding into Telesp, along with the spin-off of all of the assets of Telefonica Empresas.

In October of that year, the company set up an agreement with Abril Comunicacoes, TVA Sistema de Televisao, Comercial Cabo TV Sao Paul Ltda, TVA Sul Parana Ltda and TVA Radioenlaces Ltda, which combined Telesp's broadband and telecommunication services with the broadband and cable services of companies.

Profile

Telesp provides fixed-line telecommunications that include local services, measured service, public telephones, long-distance, multimedia services and network services.

The telephone network for Telesp has 14.4 million fixed lines, which includes public telephone lines. 74.9 percent of their access lines are of residential use, 20.3 percent are commercial, two percent are public telephones and 2.8 percent are for the company's own use. Local service include measuring service on all calls that originate or end in the local area. Telesp also has a telephone service agreement to offer local services to other states, including Sergipe, Espirito Santo, Rio Grande do Sul, Parana, Santa Catarina and parts of Rio de Janeiro.

The company also provides local telephone services in Para, Amapa, Rondonia, Maranhao, Tocantins and Acre. In May 2005, the company started providing telephone services to Ceara, Amazonas, Pernambuco, Rio de Janeiro, Bahia, Mato Grosso do Sul and Mato Grosso. A year later, services from the company began to appear in Brasilia and Goiania.

The company also has agreements that allow it to begin operations in Porto Alegre, Curitiba, Brasilia, Rio de Janeiro, Vitoria, Belo Horizonte and Salvador by supplying the infrastructure that is needed to create new generation telecom networks.

Some other services the company provides are interactive e-mail, banking services, free Internet access through I-Telefonica, which provides service to 620 cities in the state of Sao Paulo and 1,000 cities in Brazil.

In 2007, the company was granted a license to provide direct satellite distribution of television for subscribers.

Company News

In November of 2007, Telesp bought Abril Comunicacoes, Tevecap, TVA Sistema de Televisao and Rede Ajato, which was approved by the Brazilian National Agency for Telecommunications.

Telemig Celular Participacoes S.A. (TMB)

Telemig Celular Participacoes S.A. (TMB), also referred to as just Telemig, is a provider of cellular telecom services in Minas Gerais, Brazil. It offers prepaid and contract services to subscribers, in addition to business solutions for corporate users. The company is based in Belo Horizonte, Brazil and has 3.5 million customers. Telemig Celular's stock is traded on the NYSEEuronext and Bovespa. It is part of the Ibovespa index.

History

The company was formed when Brazil's govenment-owned telephone monopoly Telebras broke up into eight different companies. It was originally the wireless company for the state of Minas Gerais. It was sold by the Brazilian government in June of 1998 to a group which included Canada's Telesystem International Wireless, Brazilian bank Opportunity and six Brazilian pension funds. Telesystem International Wireless was later divested, and is currently owned by Vivo, a Brazilian joint-venture between Portugal Telecom and Telefónica of Spain.

Profile

Their services include real time play-by-play of soccer matches, fax reception through mobile handsets, call conferencing, caller line identification, and customized ring tones.

The company utilizes AMPS and IS-136 networks on the 800/850MHz band and a GSM network on the 1800MHz (DCS) band, and began a 3G (HSDPA) implementation on 850MHz in Belo Horizonte. It plans to offer state-wide 3G services by the end of 2008.

They have 48% of the market share in Minas Gerais.

Tele Norte Leste Participacoes (TNE)

Known as Oi, which is Portuguese for 'Hi', this company was formally known as Telmar and is now known as Telemar Norte Leste. Currently, it is the largest landline telephone company in Brazil, both in terms of lines of service and revenues.

With its headquarters in Rio de Janeiro, the company currently employs over 30,000 individuals across the country. The company has 15.2 million land lines in service, 5.7 million wireless customers and 400,000 ADSL subscribers.

The company provides services to 65 percent of Brazil, in Rio de Janeiro, Minas Gerais, Espirito Santo, Bahia, Sergipe, Alagoas, Pernambuco, Paraiba, Rio Grande do Norte, Piaui, Ceara, Maranhao, Para, Amazonas, Amapa and Roraima.

History of Company

The company came into being in 2006 when Telemar was restructured and merged with three other companies to create a single company. The companies were rebranded under the name 'Oi', although its full name is Telemar Norte Leste Participacoes S.A.

Profile

The company is made up of seven subsidiaries: Oi Fixo (landlines), Oi Movel (mobile), 31 (long distance), Oi Velox (ADSL), Oi Internet (ISP), Oi Voip (Voice over IP) and Oi WiFi (wireless access).

The company has over 13 million mobile subscribers to its service, while there are 1.1 million broadband subscribers. 86 percent of the company's consolidated revenues were generated through its operations in the fixed-line and data business. The mobile telecom market makes up the other 14 percent.

The local services include local calls, collect calls, in-dialing service to corporate clients and measured service.

The company provides traffic transportation services under the name Tmar, which allows international operators to terminate their Brazilian inbound traffic through the company's telecom network.

The mobile telecommunications of the company are available through 824 municipalities in 16 states, with over 13 million subscribers. Of the customer base, 82 percent of the customer base are on prepaid plans while 18 percent are on the postpaid plans. Their postpaid plans offer caller ID, voice mail, and radio service, and are paid on a subscription fee monthly basis.

The company has over 577,000 public telephones in service, all of which operate on a prepaid card.

Company News

In January of 2008, the company announced that it may possibly take over Brasil Telecom.

TIM Participacoes S.A. (TSU)

TIM Participacoes is the only company in Brazil that offers cellular service throughout the entire country through its subsidiaries, TIM Celular S.A. and TIM Nordeste S.A.

The company is also the largest global system for mobile telecommunications, in terms of both customers and revenues. Currently, the company has 29.2 million customers and a market share in excess of 25 percent.

History of Company

In 1998, the Brazilian government transferred control of Tele Celular Sul to Telepar Celular, of Telepar Celular, along with Telesc Celular and Celular S.A.

Later that year, the group of companies formed into UGB Participacoes Ltda and Bitel Participacoes S.A., and bought a controlling interest of the company from the Brazilian government during the privatization of the Telebras system.

TIM was the first company to offer Blackberry services in Brazil

In September of 1998, common and preferred stocks of Tele Celular Sul began trading on the Sao Paulo Stock Exchange. It subsequently began trading on the New York Stock Exchange.

In December 1998, UGB sold its stock in the company to Bitel Participacoes, with approval of the Brazilian Antitrust organization. the company ended up being controlled by Telecom Italia Mobile [TIM].

TIM acquired the license to operate cell phone D and E bands in Brazil in January of 2001, the only group authorized to do so. In July of 2003, the company implemented the Carrier Selection Code, which allows the customer to choose the long-distance provider. The following month, the company changes its name to TIM Sul S.A and launched the Global System for Mobile Communication.

In September 2003, the company merged with Bitel to create TIM Brasil Servicos e Participacoes. In March of 2006, the company bought TIM Celular.

Profile

TIM Participacoes is a wireless provider throughout Brazil, which uses a global system for its mobile communications technology. In four of the areas it covers, TIM offers time-division multiple access technology [TDMA] as well as GSM. The company also provides value added services including text messaging, multimedia messaging services, Blackberry services, video call and wireless application protocol. Also, the company provides interconnection services to fixed line and mobile providers.

Company News

TIM Participacoes is believed to be responsible for the increase in the overall number of Brazilians using cell phones, a 21 percent annual increase, since they control over 25 percent of the wireless market in Brazil..

Company Trivia

The company was the first to offer Blackberry services to Brazil.

Vivo Participacoes S.A. (VIV)

The largest mobile phone provider in Brazil, and South America, Vivo has 28 million subscribers. They provide voice and related services such as voicemail, call forwarding, three-way calling, caller identification, chat room, and data services.

History of Company

A relatively new company in terms of its creation, as it was incorporated in 1998, it was formed into its present form in February 2006 when Tele Leste Celular Participacoes, Tele Sudeste Celular Participacoes and Celular CRT Paticipacoes merged into one entity, with TCP being the surviving company. The company then changed their name to Vivo Participacoes.

The merger resulted from the Portugal Telecom and Telefonic-owned companies. Since then, NBT and TCO Celular were purchased later on as part of a joint venture. The amalgamation off all these companies provided coverage in Rio de Janeiro, Sao Paulo, Parana, Santa Catarina, Espirito Santo, Rio Grande do Sul, Bahia, Sergipe, Amazonas, Roraima, Para, Amapa, Maranhao, Goais, Acre, Tocantins, Mato, Grosso, Mato Grosso do Sul and the Brazilian Federal District.

Profile

The company operates through its subsidiary Vivo S.A., which is the cellular operator in Brazil, serving over 85 percent of the country. Their service is in 19 Brazilian states, reaching 7.3 million square kilometers. The company utilizes the GSM, CDMA and TDMA frequencies.

In Sao Paulo, Vivo has over 10.7 million cellular lines, and in Espirito Santo, it has 4.9 million cellular lines. The company covers 60 percent of the cities, 93 percent of the population, in Parana and Santa Catarina, with 2.8 million cellular lines in operation.

In Rio Grande do Sul, Vivo covers 70 percent of the cities and 96 percent of the residents, utilizing 3.3 million cellular lines. For the areas of Acre, Amapa, Amazonas, Goias, Tocantins, Mato, Grosso, Mato Grosso do Sul, Rondonia, Maranhao, Para and Roraima, it covers over 53 percent of the cities and in excess of 90 percent of the population, with a total of 5.9 million cellular lines. In Bahia and Sergipe, 45 percent of the cities and 78 percent of the population are covered, with 1.6 million cellular lines in use.

The company also a provider of voicemail, call forwarding, text messaging, data service and caller ID to its customers. The company also implemented three location-based services recently. The first, Vivo Localiza Familia, allows parents to locate and monitor their children using the Internet and their cell phones. Vivo Localiza Amigos is a service which allows the customer to locate friends, and be located by friends. Vivo Co-Piloto, helps customers travel through Brazilian cities.

Vivo's network is based on the IS-95/cdmaOne technology, with a portion on an analog AMPS service, or TMDA service. However, the network is being converted to CDMA2000.

Company News

In 2007, Oi bought a controlling interest in Tele Norte Celular Participacoes from Vivo, giving them over 51 percent ownership in the company.

Brazil Food Stocks

Companhia Brasileira de Distribuicao (CBD)

Commonly known as Grupo Pao de Acucar, which is the trading name of the company, this Brazilian company is engaged in the business of retailing food, electronic goods, home merchandise and other products sold in supermarkets, department stores, and home appliance stores. The company has over 63,000 employees and is headquartered out of Sao Paulo.

Currently, the company has over 550 stores in Brazil, with more than 490 operated as retail food stores. Approximately 310 of these stores are located in the State of Sao Paulo, where 58 percent of the company's sales revenue are generated. The company operates distribution centers in Sao Paulo, Rio de Janeiro, Brasilia, Fortaleza, Curtiba and Recife and other parts of Brazil.

History of Company

Founded as Doceira Pao de Acucar in 1948, the business started out as a pastry shop. The company grew to two stores in 1952, and their first supermarket opened in 1959. By 1965, the company had 11 stores and in 1966 it located a store in Santos, its first store outside of Sao Paulo.

In 1968, the store had grown to 64 stores. During that year, the company formed the International Division, which built stores of the company in Portugal, Angola and Spain.

By the 1970s, the company started building their first hypermarkets in Brazil. In 1978, the company took over Superbom, Peg-pag and Mercantil and launched its minibox stores in 1979, its stores for low-income customers. In the

1980s, the company bought six stores from Morita, five stores from Bazar, and as well as launched the first superbox stores in Jundiai and Rio de Janerio.

In the 1990s, the company reorganized itself into four different market targets, Pao de Acucar, Extra, Superbox and Eletro. In 1994, with the introduction of the Real and the lowering of inflation rates, the company saw huge growth serving as many as 19 million people. In 1995, the company had its first public stock offering. The shares initially began to trade on the Sao Paulo Stock Exchange, with the initial listing appearing on the New York Stock Exchange in 1997, which raised $172.5 million. Due to the substantial growth of the economy in Brazil, the company changed its formats to appeal to different consumer segments. The Pao de Acucar became a high-end supermarket, while the Barateiro format, which was purchased in 1998, was directed towards low-income families.

In February 1999, the company purchased the Peralta chain, which was made up of one hypermarket and 37 supermarkets. This acquisition caused the company to add 61,000 square meters of sales area and 4,800 new employees. That same year, the company partnered with Casino Group, with Casino Group acquiring 40 percent of the voting stock in the company, and 35.5 percent of the capital.

The company opened 16 new stores in 2000, as well as buying 64 more stores and adding 23 percent to their overall sales floor area, which reached 815,000 square meters. During that year, the company also opened three new distribution centers, with a total area of 350,000 square meters. The following year, the company acquired 26 stores from Supermercados, which increased sales by about 14 percent for the company due to the store locations in Rio de Janeiro. Additional acquisitions continued during the next few years, with the company increasing its total stores by several hundred.

Profile

Companhia Brasileira De Distribuicao was incorporated in 1981 as a food retailer. As of 2006, the company has most of its stores located in the Sao Paulo State, which makes up 59.6 percent of the company's revenue. The company operates its stores under six different names: Pao de Acucar (164 stores), CompreBem (186 stores), Sendas (62 stores), Extra (83 stores), Extra Electro (50 stores) and Extra Perto (four stores).

The Pao de Acucar stores operate as local neighborhood stores, located in urban areas. The stores feature baked goods, wine, meat, cheese, perishables, and seafood. Some of the stores have shopping advisors who assist customers with finding certain foods, checking prices and discounts, and providing brand comparisons and information. The size of the stores range in size from 331 to 4,730 square meters and with an average of about 1,350 square meters of selling space. In total, food represents 92.8 percent of the sales for the stores. Customers can also take advantage of an online food ordering service.

The CompreBem stores are located in lower-income neighborhoods with the stores. The store space ranges from 300 to 2,060 square meters and average 1,214 square meters. Currently non-food items are 89.9 percent of the sales.

The Senda stores were purchased when the company bought Sendas Distribuidora. These stores are targeted towards lower-income consumers, with all of the stores located in lower-income neighborhoods of Rio de Janeiro. In 2006, the company had closed three of the stores and converted one of them into a ABC CompreBem store.

The Extra hypermarkets are the largest stores that the company owns, providing 70,000 items in an area of 7,579 square meters. Currently, food makes up 61.3 percent of the sales for the company.

The Extra-Electro stores are small showroom stores which sell home appliances and consumer electronics. These stores are usually only 674 square meters in size, with customers placing orders at the store and having their products shipped to a central warehouse.

The Extra Perto Convenience Stores are between 150 and 250 square meters in size, with two check-outs and only offering essential products.

Company News

In November of 2007, the company announced it had entered into a joint venture with Assai Comercial e Importadora Ltda, to act as a cash and carry business, with the company holding 60 percent stake in Importadora.

Companhia de Bebidas Das Americas [AMBEV] (ABV)

A relatively new company, Companhia de Bebidas das Americas (AMBEV) produces and distributes beer, including draft beer, malt, soft drinks, sport drinks, ice tea and bottled water. The products are distributed throughout Brazil, in addition to 14 other countries across North and South America. The company has three divisions, beer, carbonated soft drinks and non-carbonated drinks.

The company is a marketer and distributor of Pepsi products throughout Latin America, as well as selling Lipton Ice Tea and Gatorade. The company also distributes Budweiser products in Canada, and the Brahma drink in the United States, Europe, Asia and Africa.

History of Company

The company was established on July 1, 1999 resulting from a merger between Brahma and Antarctica, which resulted in it becoming the largest private producer of consumer goods in Brazil, and the largest brewer in Latin America. Brahma is a Brazilian beer, which was originally produced by the Companhia Cervejaria Brahma, which was founded in 1888.

In 2004, AMBEV entered into a partnership with InBev, which allowed the company to operate in North America, due to a merger with Labatt, which resulted in the company becoming the Brewer of the Americas. The company has the largest selection of beverage products in Brazil.

In August of 2006, they purchased Quinsa from the Beverages Association Corporation. On April 17, 2007, the

company completed the takeover of Goldensand Comercio e
Servicos

Profile

The company has 13 mixed plants, 12 breweries, four
soft drink plants, three raw material plants, one malt plant
and a farm in the state of Amazonas. They have a 91.18
percent stake in Quinsa, which has operations in Argentina,
Bolivia, Chile, Paraguay and Uruguay, Equator, Guatemala,
El Salvador, Nicaragua, Peru, the Dominican Republic and
Venezuela. The company recently opened up a plant with a
capacity to produce one million hectorliters of beer. The
plant also created 1,350 new jobs.

Outside of the United States, AMBEV is the largest
Pepsi bottler; accounting for 69 percent of the Brazilian
beverage market, while employing 34,000 employees.
Currently, the company has one million points of sale in the
country, hundreds of third-party distributors, 16,000 trucks,
13,000 salesmen, in addition of owning and operating
numerous boats and ferries that cross the Amazon River.

In Brazil, the company sells soft drinks, iced tea and
bottled water, with the primary brands being Guarana
Antarctica Pepsi, and Lipton Ice Tea. The company's
distribution network has two branches: one is a third-party
distributor that has 200 operators, and the company's own
distributor, which has 40 distribution centers throughout
Brazil. They are a major competitor of Coca-Cola in Brazil.

The company sells the Brahva brand, which is
distributed through the Central America Bottling Corporation
in Guatemala, El Salvador and Nicaragua. In the Dominican
Republic, the company has a brewing and bottling facility for
its soft drink products that began in 2005. The primary
brands in the Dominican Republic are Red Rock, Pepsi, and
Seven Up.

AMBEV also distributes beer in Ecuador since 2003, and it also has the Brahma there.

In Peru, the company markets Concordia, Pepsi and Triple Kola, competing with SAB Miller, Cerveceria Centro Americana, Coca-Cola, Cveceria Polar and Cerveceria Regional.

In North America, the company distributes through Labatt's, which includes both domestic and InBev beer brands. The primary brands for the company in Canada are Budweiser and Bud Light, Labatt Blue, Alexander Keith's and Kokanee, and in Ontario, it partners with Molson Coors Brewing Company and Sleeman Breweries. In Quebec, the company sells products through a direct sales system. They also distribute their beer in the provinces of British Columbia, Alberta, Manitoba, Saskatchewan, Yukon Territory and Northwest Territories.

Company News

In 2007, the company announced a merger to incorporate Beverage Associates with AMBEV, in order to simplify operations and reduce costs.

Company Trivia

AMBEV is the fifth largest brewer in the world and the leading brewer in Brazil. The company distributes 12 billion liters of beverages every year in North and South America.

Perdigao S.A. (PDA)

Perdigao is a food company that specializes in poultry, pork and beef, along with processed dairy products. Their products include whole and cut chickens, frozen pork cuts and beef, processed foods, specialty meats, processed meats and pasta.

History of Company

The history of Perdigao began in 1934, when Italian immigrants started the business. During the next quarter of a century, the company has expanded into several areas, and became one of the largest food companies in Latin America.

In 2007, the company purchased Sino dos Alpes Alimentos Ltda, which is a subsidiary of Grandi Salumifici Italiani. That same year, the company purchased of Plusfood Groep, a division of Cebeco Groep, a Dutch holding company.

By the end of the year, the company acquired 51 percent of Batavia, a dairy-processing company.

Profile

Perdigao has an organizational structure of 20 industrial units througout Brazil. They have 39,000 employees and has 2,500 different products, which are sold under the brands Perdiago, Perdix, Batavo, Chester, Apreciatta, Borella, Halal, Turma da Monica, Sulina, Alnoor, Toque de Sabor, Light & Elegant, Escolha Saudavel, Confidence, Fazenda, Confianca, Unef, BFF and Nabrasa.

Operations are disbursed through a network of 24 distribution centers, 15 dairy-processing distributors and 35 cross-docking transit points in Brazil. In addition, the company has a distribution network in more than 100 countries around the world.

The operations of the company are split into poultry, pork and beef, milk, processed food products and other items, such as animal feed.

The poultry division produces frozen whole and cut chickens, quail and partridges. The company sold 530,200 tons of frozen chicken in 2006, with most being exported.

The pork and beef division produces over 143,000 tons of frozen pork cuts, loins, and ribs. Similar to the poultry, most of the pork and beef is exported around the world.

The milk division produces pasteurized and UHT milk, which is sold in Brazil. They produce about 150,000 tons of milk per year.

The processed food products division makes up a significant portion of the company's revenues, and includes marinated, frozen chicken, rooster meat, turkey meat, specialty meats, frozen foods, entrees and dairy products. The company also makes chicken hot dogs, chicken sausages and chicken bologna. The company sells about 765,000 300 tons of processed foods, most within Brazil.

The last division of the company produces animal feed for poultry and hogs, however, most of the feed is used within the company, with only four percent sold to outside customers. The company also produces some soy products.

Company News

In September of 2007, the company announced that it was building a new agro industrial complex near Recife in the Pernambuco state, with two plants to be built for diary processing and meat storage.

In December of 2007, the company purchased Eleva Alimentos.

Company Trivia

It was the first food company to be listed on the Sao Paulo stock exchange.

Sadia S.A. (SDA)

Sadia is a food producer located in Concordia, Santa Catarina, which is one of the leading producers of frozen food in the world and the primary Brazilian exporter of meat-based products.

The translation of the company's name is 'healthy' in Portuguese, which is what the company is trying to project to its customers about its food..

Sadia has 12 industrial plants which produce 1.3 million tons of meat products. They have 70,000 points of sale in Brazil and 200 foreign clients around the world.

The company became so influential that, in 2003, the former chairman of the company, Luis Fernando Furlan, was appointed Minister of Industry and Foreign Trade by President Luiz Inacio Lula da Silva.

History of Company

The company began in 1944 in Brazil, when Attilio Fontana bought a small grain mill and renamed the company Sadia. Within two years, the company had gone into the pork processing industry, and had its first sales office open up in 1951.

In 1953, the company began shipping its pork products by air, which led to the formation of the Transbrasil airline. That same year, Sadia opened a meat processing plant in Sao Paulo.

By 1956, they began chicken processing and in 1961, the company developed contracted partnerships with farmers to create vertical integration. In 1964, the company created Frigobras, a cold storage meat specialist.

The company went public in 1971 and changed its name to Sadia Concordia S.A. Industria e Comercio.

By the mid 1970's, the company begins exporting to the Middle East, which would become the largest export market for the company.

In 1992, the company began to expand throughout the rest of South America, starting with Argentina. Five years later, the company restructured itself by expanding its processed food operations and selling off its beef and soybean business.

In 1999, Sadia acquired the Miss Daisy company, and the following year the company setup a joint venture with Cargill Foods and formed Concordia Foods Ltd.

Profile

Sadia has over 2,500 products, including poultry, pork, meats, sausages, pasta, hamburgers, soups and desserts. The operational divisions include animal feed plants, breeding farms for poultry and hog stock, hatcheries, pork breeding centers, slaughterhouses, processing units, and distribution centers.

The company sells over 918,000 tons of poultry per year, over 122,000 tons of pork, and more than 800,000 tons of processed foods.

Currently, the company's operations are organized into four subsidiaries: poultry, pork, beef, and processed foods which include frozen and refrigerated products.

Company News

In December of 2007, Sadia was sued for fraud by Agritechnics Group for an apparent misappropriation of $1.4 million on a fraudulent transaction. The lawsuit was filed in George and it alleged that on Feb. 7, 2007, two attorneys for Sadia submitted a fraudulent statement to the Deutsche Bank SA Brazil.

Company Trivia

Sadia was voted the most important and valuable brand among all of Brazil's food brands in a recent Brazilian poll.

Brazil Fast Food Corporation (BOBS.OB)

Brazil Fast Food Corp, which is also referred to as Bob's, is a company that operates in Brazil as a fast food hamburger restaurant chain. The company has over 500 restaurants, which includes 181 kiosks. Bob's owns 61 of the restaurants, while the rest are owned by franchisees.

More than half of the Bob's restaurants are located in the states of Rio de Janeiro and Sao Paulo, with the rest spread throughout Brazil. Also, there are two franchised restaurants in Angola and Portugal.

Bob's has the largest amount of franchise restaurants outside of Rio de Janeiro and Sao Paulo in the states of Parana and Santa Catarina.

The company has its headquarters in Rio de Janeiro and has nearly 4,000 employees.

History of Company

The company came into existence in the early 1950's, when Robert Falkenburg, came to Brazil and introduced the fast food concept to the country's citizens. In 1951, Robert opened Falkenburg Ltd. Ice Cream, which sold vanilla ice cream with equipment and ingredients that were imported from the United States.

Then a year later, Falkenburg opened the first Bob's in Copacabana, where he created the first Brazil hotdog, hamburger and milkshake restaurant.

In 1972, Falkenburg sold the restaurant and in 1984, the company began to setup a franchise system, which lead to the expansion of hundreds of stores across Brazil.

Currently, it is a leading recognized brand in Brazil, and the primary fast foot restaurant chain in Brazil after McDonald's.

Profile

The Brazil Fast Food Corporation, owner of Bob's Restaurants, was incorporated as its current entity in 1992. All their restaurants serve a menu of hamburgers, cheeseburgers, chicken burgers, hot dogs, French fries drinks and desserts. Also, some of their restaurants even serve beer and coffee. The company utilizes the single line system, which allows customers to add various items as they go through the line, similar to a buffet style. In addition, the company cooks orders as they are received.

The restaurants are open from 10 a.m. to late evenings closing at various hours depending on the location. They are open all year round, seven days a week.

The company sells franchises, with franchisees paying R$60,000 for a restaurant, with a lower cost for kiosks. In addition, the company receives five percent of all gross sales from the franchisee. There is also a four percent sales fee, payable monthly, to cover advertising. Franchisee terms are generally five years, with the contract being renewable at the end of every term.

Besides the restaurants, the company also operates several gasoline stations including Shell and Petrobas.

Company Trivia

The founder of Bob's, Robert Falkenburg, was a tennis champion at Wimbledon from 1948 to 1949, and a three-time champion in the United States.

Brazil Utility & Forestry Stocks

CPFL Energia S.A. (CPL)

CPFL Energia is one of the largest Brazilian companies that provides electrical generation and distribution. The company has five divisions: CPFL Brasil, CPFL Pirantininga, CPFL Paulista, CPFL Geracao and SEMESA.

CPFL is headquartered in Campinas, Sao Paulo and, in terms of revenues, is the 44th largest Brazilian company.

Company History

The company can trace its beginnings back to 1912, when four small energy companies merged together in order to provide service to the interior of the State of Sao Paulo.

In 1927, American Foreign Power, incorporated the merged company CPFL Paulista, and remained a part of the organization until 1964, when it became a subsidiary of Eletrobras.

In 1975, the control of CPFL Paulista was turned over to Companhia Energetica de Sao Paulo, a company that was controlled by the Sao Paulo state government. In 1997, the company was privatized.

The company expanded in 2002, and CPFL Energia became the controlling company. In 2004, the company went public with its first Initial Public Offering.

The company continued with organizational changes in 2005, with CPFL Energia turning CPFL Geracaos into CPFL Energia's wholly owned subsidieary. That same year, the company acquired Clion Assessoria e Comercializacao de Energia Electrica Ltda. Then in 2007, the company bought CMS Energy Brasil and Rio Grande Energia S.A.

Profile

The company is in the business of producing and distributing electricity to both commercial and residential customers and providing electric-related services to affiliates.

They distribute 26,679 gigawatts of electricity to 4.5 million customers in the state of Sao Paulo, and their subsidiary, Rio Grande Energia, provides 6,787 gigawatts of electricity to 1.1 million customers in the state of Rio Grande do Sul. The company's revenue distribution is as follow 31.4 percent from industrial customers, 19.6 percent from commercial customers, 37.3 percent from residential customers, 3.3 percent from rural customers, with the balance of 8.4 percent from other customers.

CPFL has an installed capacity of in excess of 1,072 megawatts. The company also owns 23 small hydroelectric generation plants and one thermoelectric power plant.

Trivia

CPFL Energia was the first Brazilian company to simultaneously trade on the Sao Paulo Stock Exchange and on the New York Stock Exchange as a Level III ADR.

Companhia de Saneamento Basico do Estado de Sao Paulo [SABESP] (SBS)

Sabesp is a Brazilian utility company which provides water and sewage services to 367 municipalities in Sao Paulo, which includes the City of Sao Paulo. Their customer base includes residential, commercial, government, and industrial customers.

The sanitation services it provides include collection, treatment, and processing of sewage. They supply water to various municipalities in the Sao Paulo Metropolitan Region.

The company, which is headquartered in Sao Paulo, Brazil has 17,000 employees.

History of Company

The company came about through the concern about sanitation in the state of Sao Paulo. In the early 1970s, the infant mortality rate in Sao Paulo went from 81.3 per thousand children born at the beginning of the decade to 87 per thousand children in 1973. It was then that the government created a commission to promote studies to analyze the state's sanitation services.

On June 29, 1973, Sabesp was created to operate basic sanitation services throughout the State of Sao Paulo.

By 1978, the infant mortality rate had dropped to 70.6 per thousand children. Ten years later, the rate was down to 38.5 per thousand, and by 1993, it was 28.4 per thousand children.

In the early 1990s, Sabesp faced a series of financial crises of unpaid debts, increased short-term borrowings, lack of enough water to serve all the residents, and disagreements with other territories, resulting in financial losses.

In 1995, after various organizational changes, the company was able to provide water to 100 percent of citizens who had water lines, and expanded sewage collector to 85 percent of the residents in their service network.

Currently, Sabesp operates in 368 communities, supplying water to approximately 23 million people.

Profile

Sabesp operates out of the State of Sao Paulo, constructing and operating water, sewage and industrial wastewater systems in that area.

The company has 800 production units, and in order to maintain water quality and quantity, they perform 147 thousand water analyses each month, utilizing 15 laboratory centers.

The company's water division provides over 2.8 billion cubic meters of water each year to its customers, utilizing 20 reservoirs of non-treated water and 182 reservoirs of treated water, located in eight water producing systems.

The company can treat 67.7 cubic meters of water per second, and are planning an upgrade in 2009 which would allow them to treat up to 75.2 cubic meters per second.

Currently, the Cantareira, Guarapiranga and Alta Tiete systems supply 84 percent of the water produced in the region, with the Cantareira providing about half of that supply. The company has 197 water treatment facilities, and all the water treated by the company receives fluoridation treatment.

Their water distribution system has over 61,000 kilometers of water pipes and water mains, and 6.6 million water connections, with about 90 percent of the water pipes made with cast iron or polyvinylchloride.

Just in the Sao Paulo Metro Region alone, there are over 31,000 kilometers of pipes and water mains, and 373 storage tanks.

The sewage system of the company collects 82 percent of all the sewage produced in the Sao Paulo Metro Region and 71 percent produced in the Regional Systems. The sewage system is made of clay pipes and polyvinylchloride pipes.

The Sewage Treatment and Disposal division collects 58 percent of the sewage in the Sao Paulo Metro Region and 73 percent in the Regional Systems, which is approximately 63 percent of all the sewage collected in the state. Treated water is discharged into the Atlantic Ocean and inland waterways.

The company has 438 sewage treatment facilities and 44 sludge treatment facilities, with the five largest located in the Sao Paulo Metro Region. There are also 354 secondary treatment facilities in the Interior Region. The company produces over 53,000 tons of dry base sludge per year is disbursed into landfills and farmland.

Company News

In 2007, Sabesp was chosen by over half of the readers of Saneamento Ambiental as the best Sanitation Company of the Year for 2007. The prize was given due to the company's expansion of water and sewage services and its coverage area, the conservation, modernization, and the company's environmental policy.

The company announced in December of 2007 that it had started construction new wastewater treatment plants in Bertioga, Cubatao, Santos, Sao Vincente and Guaruja, with most of the funding coming from the Japan Bank for

International Cooperation. Project completion is expected in 2010, with over 1,100 kilometers of sewerage trunk lines and interceptors, more than 120,000 new home connections, over 100 sewerage pumping plants, and seven water treatment stations. It will serve 1.6 million people, and the sewerage coverage of the coastal cities of Sao Paulo will increase from 53 percent to 95 percent.

Company Trivia

The company produces 100 thousand liters of water per second, which is supplied to 25 million customers, 80 percent of the population of the State of Sao Paulo. If you took the company's network of pipes and put them all in a row, they could stretch around the world twice!

Companhia Energetica de Minas Gerais [CEMIG] (CIG)

Companhia Energetica de Minas Gerais, also known as CEMIG, is the largest combined power generator and distributor in Brazil, with over 50 power plants and a generating capacity of 6,000 megawatts. The company is also in the business of providing cable television and Internet and telecommunications services.

Company History

The origins of the company started in 1952, when the Gafanhoto power plant was built by the state government. The power plant was a significant factor in the growth of Contagem, the largest industrial region in Minas Gerais.

Later on, additional power plants were built including the Itutinga, Piau, Salto, Grande Cajuru and Tres Marias. In the 1960s, the company received support from the U.N. Development Program and the World Bank to improve the potential of the river basins in the state, leading to the construction of the Jaguara, Volta Grande, Sao Simao, Emborcacao and Nova Ponte Power Plants.

The company now has the Queimado, Aimores, Pai Joaquim and Irape power plants under construction.

Over half of the stock in Cemig is owned by Minas Gerais, which his traded on the Bovespa and the New York Stock Exchange.

Profile

CEMIG is a power generation company which has 51 hydroelectric plants, four thermoelectric plants and one wind farm. Eight of the hydroelectric plants produce over 82 percent of the electrical generation of the company. The Ipatinga Power Plant is operated by the subsidiary, Usina Termica Ipatinga, and has a generating capacity of 40 megawatts. The company also operates the Sa Carvalho Power Plant through the Sa Carvalho subsidiary and the Rosal Power Plant is operated through Rosa Energia S.A.

The company also has the Horizontes Energia subsidiary which generates electricity through the Machado Mineiro Power Plant, the Salto do Paraopeba Power Plant and the Salto do Passo Velho Power Plant.

The company transmits electricity through 1,352 miles of 500 kilovolt power lines, 1,202 miles of 345 kilovolt power lines and 467 miles of 230 kilovolt lines, utilizing 33 substations, with 97 transformers that have a transformation capacity of 15,393 megavolts.

The company generates its own energy, and also purchases power from Itaipu. CEMIG has 12 industrial consumers which account for about 20 percent of the total amount of electricity the company sells.

In addition to electrical generation, the company also produces and markets natural gas. Through its Gasmig subsidiary, they supply 2 million cubic meters of gas per day. They also provide half a million cubic meters of gas per day to thermal power plants and 1.5 million cubic meters of gas per day to retail costumers. Currently, the company owns 55 percent of Gasmig.

Empresa de Infovias, another division, has an optical fiber-based telecommunications network which is integrated into the company's power grid. Its broadband and telecommunication services are utilized in Belo Horizonte, Pocos de Caldas and barbacena, Contagem, Sete Lagoas, Ipatinga and Uberaba.

Company News

On January 10, 2008, the company had the winning bid for the Santo Antonio hydropower project that will be built on the Madeira River. The first two of the 44 units are expected to be up and running by December of 2012.

Companhia Paranaense de Energia [COPEL] (ELP)

Companhia Paranaense de Energia, also known as COPEL, is an electric power company that generates, transmits, and distributes electricity in Brazil's Parana state. The company also provides telecommunication and information technology services through various partnerships.

The company has 17 hydroelectric plants and one thermoelectric plant that generate about 4,550 megawatts, 99.6 percent of which is hydroelectric. The company has 7,210 kilometer of transmission lines and 165,757 kilometers of distribution lines throughout Brazil.

Company History

Copel was formed on October 29, 1954 after a decree was signed by Governor Bento Munhoz da Rocha Netto. Under the decree, Copel all power generation, transmission, distribution and marketing was centralized. Subsequently, Copel began building interconnection systems and constructing hydropower projects.

In the 1960s, the company started operating the Figueira Thermal Power Plant, and in 1967 the company started producing electricity from the Salto Grande do Iguacu Power Plant.

By 1970, the Julio de Mesquita Filho Power Plant was launched to serve the western regions of the state. The company started up the Capivari-Cachoeira Power Plant in 1971 which was the largest facility, at that time.

In 1980, Copel brought the Foz do Areia Hydroelectric Power Plant online, which allowed the company to reach 2.9 billion kWh, one billion higher than the previous year.

During the 1980s and 1990s, the power demand dramatically increased, so the company started up the Segredo Power Plant and Salto Caxias Hydoelectric Plant, which helped reduce the state's dependence on energy from other states.

Profile

COPEL is an electric utility that is made up of five subsidiaries, Copel Geracao, Copel Transmissao, Copel Distribuicao, Copel Telecomunicacaes and Copel Participacaes.

The company generates electricity through 18 power plants, with a total capacity of 4,549 megawatts. In 2006, the company generated over 10,000 gigawatts per hour. The operational headquarters is based in the city of Curitiba, and utilizes 12 substations, 11 of which are remote-operated.

The transmission division builds, runs, and maintains all the substations that are used in electrical transmissions, as well as maintains power lines. The company has 36 customers who are supplied directly with high voltage power through direct connections to its transmission lines. This division accounts for 9.5 percent of the total volume of electricity sold by Copel.

The company provided electricity to 98 percent of the state of Parana, serving 3.3 million customers, consisting of 34.5 kilovolt lines and substations.

The company also has interests in sanitation, gas supply and telecommunication and services through partnerships with other companies. In addition, Copel provides telecommunication services to 170 communities in Parana, amounting to 80 percent of the states population.

Company News

In October of 2007, Hedging-Griffo Corretora de Valores bought a 3.27 percent stake in Copel.

In January of 2008, the company acquired Sanedo Participacoes, which owns a 30 percent stake in Domino Holdings.

Company Trivia

Copel is one of the 250 largest power companies in the world.

Aracruz Celulose (ARA)

Aracruz Celulose, which is based in Sao Paulo, is one of the major manufactures of pulp in Brazil, and is the world's leading supplier of eucalyptus pulp. Their shares are traded on the Sao Paulo, New York and Madrid stock exchanges.

There are four major shareholders which control the company and its voting shares, Safra Group, Lorentzen, Votorantim and the Brazilian National Economic and Development Bank.

History of Company

The company began operations in January of 1967, when they planted their first eucalyptus plantations. In 1978, the first production mill was launched. In February 1991, the company's second production mill was built and was named Mill 'B".

In May of 1992, the company's ADR Level 3 shares were listed on the New York Exchange, and the following year it achieved its ISO 9002 certification, and later received an ISO 9001 for all its activities in 1995. By 1996, their electro-chemical plant received an ISO 9002 certification.

The company expanded into solid wood products including lyptus in March of 1997. Then in October of 2000, the company purchased a 45 percent share in the Veracel pulp mill project, and in July of 2003, the company acquired Riocell.

The company has run into trouble with environmentalists recently, due to land disputes with the Tupiniquim and Quilombolo people, and accused Aracruz of environmental damage from the planting of eucalyptus monocultures.

Profile

Aracruz Celulose is a producer and exporter of bleached hardwood market pulp with three production facilities in Brazil. They produce eucalyptus pulp used in paper and other products, including tissues, packaging boards and specialty papers.

The Barra do Riacho Unit in Espirito Santo, which produces bleach, dry and bale lines, utilizes 359,000 hectares, where 212,000 hectares are plantations and 126,000 hectares are native reserves. Their pulp production facilities are based near the port facility of Barra do Riacho, which is 51 percent owned by the company.

The Guaiba Unit in Guaiba, has a capacity of 430,000 tons of bleached eucalyptus kraft pulp, where there are 104,000 hectares of forestry, of which 66,000 are plantations and 28,000 hectares are native reserves.

The company also holds a 50 percent stake in the Veracel plant, based in Eunapolois, where over 2,600,000 tons of pulp are produced each year, amounting to 26 percent of the worldwide supply.

The company has established a joint venture with Gutchess International Group to create the Tecflor Industrial Company, which manufactures solid wood products.

Aracruz owns a sawmill in the state of Bahia, where renewable, hardwood lumber is produced from eucalyptus trees. The mill can produce 44,000 cubic meters per year. Also, the company has 11 sales representatives in major furniture markets across Brazil servicing 150 manufacturers.

The company's primary pulp mill is located in the State of Espirito Santo, with a maximum capacity of two million tons of pulp per year.

Company News

On January 11, 2008, the company reported that its fourth-quarter results for 2007 dropped by 36 percent due to higher production costs, taxes and fluctuation. They also did a record 843,000 tons of sales volume during the year.

The company also announced that, over the next five years, it would be buying land, planting trees and building new factories at a cost of R$3.5 billion.

Votorantim Celulose e Papel (VCP)

One of the largest pulp and paper companies in Brazil, Votorantim Celulose e Papel, manufactures printing and writing paper, coated paper, tissues, labels and thermal paper. Votorantim owns two paper and pulp mills located in Jacarei and Luiz Antonio, and two paper mills in Guaiba and Eunapolis. In addition to selling throughout Brazil, Votorantim also markets and exports its products internationally.

The company has their own forestry operations which provides materials for the production of paper.

The company has two other subsidiaries, Newark Financial Inc. and Normus Empreendimentos e Participacoes Ltd.

History of Company

Jose Ermirio de Moraes, founder of Grupo Votorantim, planted 80 million eucalyptus saplings in Capao Bonito In the 1950s, which launched the beginning of the company.

Over the years, the Grupo Votorantim invested in many different paper and cellulose businesses, moving heavily into the paper industry and away from the coal industry that they were involved in.

In 1995, the group aggregated all of the company's mills into one entity. The mills included Papel Simao, Votorantim Celulose e Papel and Celulose e Papel Votorantim, and the resulting company was VCP Votorantim Celulose e Papel.

Profile

This major paper manufacturer produces pulp from its forestry operations for use in its own paper production. The company sells its hardwood bleached market pulp to Brazilian markets, as well as internationally. Votorantim also manufactures coated and uncoated printing, writing paper, and specialty papers.

In 2006, the company was producing 1,480,000 tons of pulp per year, along with 640,000 tons per year of coated, uncoated and specialty papers. 37 percent of the volume and 52 percent of the sales were generated domestically. With regards to the pulp market, 12 percent of the sales volume and 11 percent of the revenues were domestic market, with a large majority coming from the international markets. For the paper market, the domestic market was 72 percent of the sales volume, while 79 percent of the revenues were domestic.

The company produces 1.4 million tons of eucalyptus pulp each year and sells over 941,000 tons of its production to third party producers.

The company manufactures 670,000 tons of paper each year.

The coated paper produced by the company is used for the production of labels and magazine covers, and uncoated paper is used with books, notebooks, and forms.

The company's wood comes from its lumber in 225,000 hectares of land in the state of Sao Paulo, along with occasional purchases of wood from third parties, about 26 percent, to use in its pulp mills.

Company News

On November 29, 2007, CEO Jose Luciano Penido of Votorantim won the Latin American CEO of the Year Award at the RISI's Second Latin American Pulp and Paper Conference. This was the first time that RISI, the largest international information agency for forestry products, had chosen someone from Latin America.

Company Trivia

Net income quadrupled between 2006 and 2007

Brazil Airline Stocks

EMBRAER - Empresa Brasileira de Aeronáutica S.A. (ERJ)

The aviation manufacturer, Empresa Brasileira de Aeronáutica S.A., which is more commonly known as EMBRAER, is the largest exporter in Brazil, the third largest in terms of annual commercial aircraft delivery, and has the fourth largest workforce among all aircraft manufacturers. The company has its headquarters, and production and design facilities in Sao Jose dos Campos, Sao Paulo. They operate maintenance and commercial sites in several countries, including the United States, China, Singapore, and France.

The company has approximately 23,770 employees.

Company History

EMBRAER came into existence on July 29, 1969, when the Ministry of Aeronautics established the company, with 500 employees and engineers from other aircraft manufacturers. The company began building two Bandeirante aircraft each month, with the first group of planes completed in February of 1973. The planes were purchased by the Brazilian Air Force, and the Transbrasil bought the first Bandeirante planes that same year.

EMBRAER started exporting planes in 1975, which resulted in 500 planes being sold to 36 countries around the world.

The next model the company produced was the Aermacchi MB-326 trainer aircraft, which was later renamed the Xavante. They also came out with the Ipanema agriculture aircraftwhich is still being produced, with 1,000 planes sold so far. 186 Xavantes were built and sold by the company over an 11 year period.

The company also built its first pressurized plane, the Xingu, in 1975. About 30 were manufactured and sold to the French Air Force in 1981.

The Tucano, the company's first combat plane, was produced in 1980, which became the most successful turboprop military training aircraft, with 650 units sold around the world.

The company started to produce the Brasilia, a regional airliner, in May of 1985. After 350 planes were sold, production ended in 2002.

In 1981, Embraer started working with Aeritalia and Aermacchi, developing an AMX fighter, to replace old military aircraft in Brazil and Italy. The first AMX flew in 1985.

The company ran into problems in 1990 when they created the CBA 123 Vector. None of the planes were ever sold in spite of the great technology.

The company incurred massive staff cuts between 1990 and 1994, dropping from 12,600 employees in 1990 to 3,200 in 1994. That same year, the company was privatized.

The company then developed a modern light attack aircraft and trainer, called Super Tucano, which flew in 1999 and was marketed to the Brazilian and Colombian air forces. The company also started construction the E-Jets series in 1990, which first flew in 2002.

Presently, the company is developing mission systems for air and ground operations for Brazil, Greece, India, and Mexico.

Profile

EMBRAER primarily manufacturers commercial aircraft, and is the supplier of defense aircraft to the Brazilian

Air Force. Also, the company sells planes to the military of countries in Europe, Asia and Latin America.

The commercial aviation division of the company develops, produces and sells jets to the airline industry worldwide. The company's products include the ERJ 145 family, the Embraer 170/190 family and the EMB 120 Brasilia family. Revenues of commercial aviation represented 64.4 percent of the company's business.

They also produce defense and government planes, and provide support for military aircraft. The company makes the Super Tucano for defense and the AL-X attack aircraft. The AMX is a ground attack jet. The company's defense and government business sector represents six percent of the total company's revenues.

The executive jet division includes the Legacy 600, Phenom 100, Phenom 300 and Lineage 1000. This division comprises 15.3 percent of the company's sales.

The customer service division provides after-sales customer support, maintenance, training, leasing, and marketing spare aircraft parts.

They also manufacture propeller aircraft and crop dusters, with this division making up 14.3 percent of the net sales of the company.

Company News

In 2007, the company reported that LOT Polish Airlines, the first carrier in Europe to use Embraer's E-jet, had agreed to buy 12 Embraer-175 regional jets at a total cost of $372 million. This agreement included two options and 10 purchase rights, which amounts to a total cost of $744 million.

The company recently announced that it had delivered 169 commercial and executive jets in 2007, a 30 percent increase over 2006, which was an all time record for the company.

Embraer announced in December of 2007 that Flight Options in the United States bought 100 executive jets amounting to an order of $746 million.

Company Trivia

The company has a facility with a 16,400-foot (five-kilometer) long runway, which is the third-longest runway in the entire world.

GOL Linhas Areas Inteligentes S.A. (GOL)

The low-cost airline GOL Linhas Areas Inteligentes S.A., also known as Gol Linhas Aereas, is the second largest airline in Brazil, with a 38.6 percent share of the domestic market, and 12.2 percent of the market of Brazilian based international airlines.

It owns Varig Airlines, with its primary hubs located at the Sao Paulo's Congonhas International Airport, Rio de Janeiro's Galeao International Airport, Brasilia International Airport, as well as operations at Rio de Janeiro's Santo Dumont Airport, Sao Paulo's Guarulhos International Airport and Porto Alegre's Salgado Filho International Airport. The company currently has about 5,500 employees.

Company History

The company began operating on January 15, 2001 as a subsidiary of Grupo Aurea, which is owned by the Constantino family. The low fares of Gol brought about strong growth in the domestic air travel market, and by 2004 the company had over 11.6 million passengers, and had a market share of 20 percent of the country's travel market.

In 2004, the company went public on the New York and Sao Paulo stock exchanges.

In March 2007, the company bought Varig for $320 million, with the company continuing with its current name.

Profile

GOL offers 630 daily flights to 58 destinations throughout Brazil, along with destinations in Argentina, Bolivia, Chili, Paraguay, Peru and Uruguay through its VRG

Linhas Aereas brand. The Gol Transportes Aereos brand provides 120 flights to 12 destinations, including Brasilia, Belo Horizonte, Curitiba, Fortaleza, Fernando de Noronha, Florianopolis, Manaus, Porto Alegre, Recife, Rio de Janeiro, Salvador and Sao Paulo.

GOL tickets can be purchased through Aerolineas Argentinas, Continental and Delta Airlines, however, Gol does not sell tickets for partner flights.

Company News

Gol Linhas Aereas announced that their VRG Linhas Aereas subsidiary would eventually provide long-haul services from Brazil to Paris and Madrid.

On January 15, 2008, the company celebrated its seventh year in business and the transportation of 75 million customers. They also announced it had reached a 40 percent domestic share in December 2007, and their load averages were 70 percent.

On January 23, 2008, the company reported that it had an agreement with KLM Royal Dutch Airlines which would allow Royal Dutch customers to buy tickets for all 60 destinations served by Gol in South America.

TAM S.A. (TAM)

TAM is a Brazilian airline that provides air transportation within the country, as well as internationally, through its subsidiaries, TAM Linhas Aereas and Transport Aereos del Mercosur. They fly to 48 cities in Brazil, with 26 additional destinations are served through partnerships with other airlines. The company also has passenger and cargo flights to 12 international destinations.

Each year, the company flies over 23 million passengers on domestic flights, and 2.6 million on international flights. Their leased fleet of aircraft includes the A330, A320 and the A319.

Company History

The company was founded by Captain Rolim Adolfo Amaro in 1961, who had formerly worked as a mechanic's assistant and messenger. When he was only 21 years old, he became a pilot for Taxi Aereo Marilia (TAM), and with an association of 10 young pilots, they flew passengers and cargo to Parana, Sao Paulo and Matto Grosso.

Six years later, he left the company, which was then sold to Orlando Ometto, who moved the headquarters to Sao Paulo and turned the company into a parcel carrier.

In 1971, Amaro returned to the company after Ometto asked him to become a minority owner with 33 percent ownership. At that time, the company was transporting only 3,000 passengers. Within one year, Amaro owned half of the company's stock and took over control of management. In 1976, he owned 67 percent of the company. Most airlines were growing at 15 percent a year, yet TAM was growing at 70 percent every six months.

In 1979, Amaro took over the entire company and by 1981, the company transported one million passengers. TAM also bought Votec Airlines in 1986, to increase service to central, eastern and northern parts of Brazil, in addition to linking the main airports with Congonhas as the hub.

In 1993, the company started Fidelidade, the frequent flyer program that made the airline a pioneer among carriers in Brazil.

By 1996, the company was serving all of Brazil, and the next year the company purchased 150 airplanes from airlines in Europe. Three years later, the company began flying to Miami, and in 2000 they started offering flights to Paris. The following year, service began to Buenos Aires and Frankfurt.

In 2001, the company's founder Amaro died in a helicopter accident in July, and two months later September 11 heavily impacted the aviation industry. However, the company was still able to grow by 31 percent and transporting 13 million passengers.

Profile

TAM is a Brazilian airline with 702 take-offs per day and transports 25 million passengers on domestic and international flights every year. The company has 95 leased aircraft that are used in the transportation of passengers, its primary business.

Due to its partnerships with Oceanair, Pantanal, Passaredo, Total Linhas and Trip Transporte, the company transports to 26 destinations around the world.

TAM has 217 international flights on a weekly basis to Miami, New York, London, Paris, Buenos Aires, Santiago, Asuncion, Montevideo, Ciudad del Este, Santa Cruz de la Sierra, and Cochabamba. Passenger transport accounts for about 94 percent of the company's revenue.

The cargo operations of the company account for slightly more than 6 percent of the company's revenue, which includes express packages, standard cargo and special transportation delivery. There are 400 Brazilian cities where the airline picks up packages, which they transport to 3,450 locations throughout the country. The company transports over 40,000 tons of cargo each year outside of Brazil.

Company News

On January 9, 2008 the company reported that it had had a 13.2 percent increase in domestic airline share over 2006.

On January 30, the company entered into a partnership with 64 airlines to provide connections to every country in South America, North America, Europe, the Middle East, Africa, Asia and Oceania.

Company Trivia

In July 17, 2007, the deadliest plane crash in Latin America occurred on a TAM Airbus A320, when the plane overran a runway at the Congonhas Airport in Porto Alegre, and hitting a TAM Express warehouse. 198 people died on the plane and on the ground.

Online Resources

The following are various online resources where you can find additional information on Brazilian stocks.

Stockerblog.com

WallStreetNewsNetwork.com

Stockpickr.com

TheStreet.com

SeekingAlpha.com

Finance.Yahoo.com

Finance.Google.com

ADR.com

www.ingramcontent.com/pod-product-compliance
Lightning Source LLC
Chambersburg PA
CBHW031811190326
41518CB00006B/286